Care Matters:
Time for Change

Presented to Parliament
by the Secretary of State for Education and Skills
by Command of Her Majesty
June 2007

Cm 7137

Contents

Foreword	3
Executive Summary	5
Chapter 1 – Corporate parenting: getting it right	14
Chapter 2 – Family and parenting support	30
Chapter 3 – Care placements: a better experience for everyone	44
Chapter 4 – Delivering a first class education	65
Chapter 5 – Promoting health and wellbeing	88
Chapter 6 – Transition to adulthood	107
Chapter 7 – The role of the practitioner	124
Chapter 8 – Next steps	135

100七429384

Foreword

Every child requires love, care and stability when they are growing up, but not all children are fortunate enough to have a loving family which is capable of providing this support. Children in care are frequently in greater need, but paradoxically less likely to receive the help they require. Many of them suffer terrible abuse and neglect before entering into a State care system that can seem cold and aloof.

We are determined to improve the plight of children in care. The aspiration that the State has for these children should be no less than each parent would have for their own child. We must ensure that they receive the security, support and schooling they need to reach their full potential and lead a happy and fulfilled life.

Investment has increased – central Government investment is now £600 million a year more than in 1997; we have taken steps to promote adoption as an option over care for some children; and we have put a duty on local authorities to promote educational achievement for children in care. There has been substantial progress thanks to the many dedicated people working in this area, but much more needs to be done.

Over the next four years, we will invest over £300 million more to ensure that children in care get a better start in life. We will clarify the responsibilities of social workers, and enable them to devote more one to one time to children in their care. We will ensure that care placements are stable, with better training and support for carers to cope with children who may be facing multiple difficulties, 24 hours a day, 7 days a week if necessary.

Education is crucial. Too often, a child in care will possess innate talents or abilities that are squandered through system failures. We will improve opportunities at every stage: particularly in the crucial early years, ensuring that they have the opportunity to go to the best schools, and to aspire to university with an additional £2,000 bursary for young people in care in higher education. It is also essential to improve access to opportunities for work with the provision of training and apprenticeships.

We will work closely with Primary Care Trusts and other key partners to improve the overall health and wellbeing of children and young people in care. We will ensure that children in care get a softer landing into adulthood, instead of being pushed out too early by the system. The average child leaves their parental home at the age of 24, yet a quarter of children in care will leave at the age of 16. We will support young people for longer – well into their twenties if necessary. Young people who have been in care should be entitled to much more – with personal support from their carers and others until they are properly ready to make the transition to adulthood.

I would like to thank the many children and young people, organisations, carers and professionals who have helped shape these proposals. For too long, this issue was out of sight and out of mind. We have now elevated the plight of these vulnerable children, harnessing the passion and commitment which exists on the ground to transform once and for all the experiences and prospects of children in care.

Rt Hon Alan Johnson MP,
Secretary of State for Education and Skills

Executive Summary

Despite high ambitions and a shared commitment for change, outcomes for children and young people in care have not sufficiently improved. There remains a significant gap between the quality of their lives and those of all children. Tackling this requires urgent, sustained action across central and local government, from practitioners in all aspects of children and young people's lives and from their carers, friends and family. The support we have had for this work has shown us that this drive and commitment exists across the country and at every level of children's services.

This White Paper sets out the steps that we will take, together with local delivery partners, to improve the outcomes of children and young people in care. It builds on responses to the Green Paper *Care Matters: Transforming the Lives of Children and Young People in Care* and the conclusions of four working groups established to investigate best practice in supporting those in care. In delivering this White Paper we will work in partnership with local government, the voluntary and private sector and the wider children's workforce to ensure that we achieve lasting change for this important group.

1. Children and young people in care[1] tell us that they want to lead normal lives. They want to succeed in education, enjoy a wide range of positive activities and make a successful transition to adult life. First and foremost, those in care are children and young people. We must have high ambitions and expectations for them. We must help them to reach their potential by providing excellent parenting, a high quality education, opportunities to develop their talents and skills, and effective support for their transition to adulthood.

2. Unfortunately, circumstances outside their control mean that children and young people in care face a number of barriers to achieving this aim. As a result of their experiences they have often had a disrupted education, they may have difficulties with their social and emotional wellbeing, and they often lack stable relationships in their lives,

---

1 This White Paper uses the term 'children in care' to include all children being looked after by a local authority, including those subject to care orders under section 31 of the Children Act 1989, and those looked after on a voluntary basis through an agreement with their parents under section 20 of the Children Act 1989

resulting in attachment problems and a lack of resilience. It is vital that carers and other professionals give children and young people in care the encouragement and support necessary for them to overcome these barriers and succeed.

3. We have already taken a number of important steps to improve the lives of children and young people in care. However, despite improvements in outcomes in recent years, there remains a gap between the outcomes of those in care and outcomes for all children:

    - In 2006, only 12% of children in care achieved 5 A*-C grades at GCSE (or equivalent) compared to 59% of all children;

    - Their health is poorer than that of other children. 45% of children in care are assessed as having a mental health disorder compared with around 10% of the general population;

    - Over 50% of children in care responding to *Care Matters* said that they had difficulties accessing positive activities;

    - 9.6% of children in care aged 10 or over, were cautioned or convicted for an offence during the year – almost 3 times the rate for all children of this age; and

    - 30% of care leavers aged 19 were not in education, employment or training (NEET).

4. It is vital that, as part of creating a socially just society, we improve this situation and narrow the gap between those in care and their peers. Some groups of children are over-represented in the care population – for example, disabled children, and some ethnic minority groups. It is important that reform is taken forward in a way that reflects this diversity.

5. Children and young people in care have a unique place in society. They have a special relationship with the State due to the fact that they have been taken into care either through a court order or by voluntary agreement with their birth parents. Central government, local authorities and their partners in children's trusts, individual professionals and carers all share responsibility for ensuring the best for children and young people in care – as they would for their own children. Children in care should be *cared about*, not just cared for.

6. The difficulties faced by those in care cannot be overcome by any individual or part of the system acting alone. It requires a coordinated approach across the whole of the children's trust. As corporate parents, we must champion the needs of children in care and deliver the best for them.

7. Through Every Child Matters, local areas are reforming the support that they provide to children, young people and families. Services are being integrated around their needs and provided through new multi-agency arrangements to support vulnerable children and young people with better prevention and earlier intervention. This

support is central to improving outcomes for children in care. In some cases it prevents the need for a child to be taken into care by enabling family and friends to meet their needs; in others it ensures that problems are minimised and are addressed effectively through good early support.

Corporate parenting: getting it right

8. Improving the role of the corporate parent, as part of children's trusts, is key to improving the outcomes for children in care. It is with the corporate parent that responsibility and accountability for the wellbeing and future prospects of children in care ultimately rest. A good corporate parent must offer everything that a good parent would, including stability. It must address both the difficulties which children in care experience and the challenges of parenting within a complex system of different services. Equally, it is important that children have a chance to shape and influence the parenting they receive. To improve the role of the corporate parent we are:

- **Expecting every local authority to put in place arrangements for a *'Children in Care Council'*, with direct links to the Director of Children's Services and Lead Member.** This will give children in care a forum to express their views and influence the services and support they receive;

- **Expecting every local authority to set out its 'Pledge' to children in care.** The pledge will cover the services and support children in care should expect to receive;

- **Making clear that the Director of Children's Services and Lead Member for Children's Services should be responsible for leading improvements in corporate parenting;**

- **Disseminating Government-funded corporate parenting training materials**, developed by the National Children's Bureau, to help authorities to ensure that effective arrangements are in place locally;

- **Introducing an Annual Stocktake of the outcomes for children in care.** This national Ministerial event will review progress for children in care with key stakeholders and representatives of local government, health services and young people in care; and

- **Introducing a three year programme of proportionate inspection**, led by Ofsted, of how local authorities are improving outcomes for children in care.

Family and parenting support

9. Wherever possible we should support children within their own families. This requires a focus on support for parents and the provision of evidence-based parenting programmes and short breaks for families with more complex needs. For those children and young people who need to be cared for

outside their immediate family, we should, at all relevant stages of the care planning process, explore the potential for enabling children to live with or be supported by wider family and friends. To achieve this we are:

- **Asking all local authorities to analyse the profile of their children in care population to ensure that appropriate services for children in care and those vulnerable children living with their families are available;**

- **Funding the development of Multi-systemic Therapy (MST) as an effective specialist intervention for older children and young people on the edge of care;**

- **Providing £280 million to deliver a step change in the availability of provision of short breaks for parents of disabled children** to reduce family stress and ensure they are better supported in their families, as set out in *Aiming Higher for Disabled Children*;

- **Legislating to enable carers who are relatives and not local authority foster carers to apply for a residence order if the child has lived with him/her for a continuous period of at least one year and to apply for residence orders to last until the child is 18; and**

- **Setting out how effective care planning will ensure that children's services continue to work with birth parents while the child is in care and that**

appropriate services are delivered for the child and family to support a child or young person's safe return home.

Care Placements: a better experience for everyone

10. A successful, stable placement is central to supporting the needs of children in care. Carers are at the centre of a child or young person's experience of corporate parenting and should provide the mainstay of their support. To improve the quality of placements for children in care, we are:

- **Improving local authority commissioning of placements, in particular by piloting Regional Commissioning Units.** This will ensure that a menu of appropriate placements, which has been tailored to meet the needs of the child, is available when placement decisions are being made;

- **Strengthening the statutory framework so that a local authority cannot place a child out of their local area unless it is satisfied that such a placement is in the child's best interests.** The authority must ensure that all children placed out of authority receive the same level of support as if they were placed closer to home;

- **Improving foster care by setting clear standards outlining the skills that all foster carers should have and increasing access to specialist training and support.** Foster carers are central to many children and young people's experience of care. It is essential that we value and support them and ensure that they are properly equipped with the necessary range of skills;

- **Revising the National Minimum Standards for foster and residential care and ensuring better enforcement of these standards** to improve the quality of provision for children and young people in care;

- **Introducing an explicit requirement for all children in care to be visited by their social worker, regardless of their placement type.** Visits can make a real difference to the children concerned, but we know that at present they do not always take place as often as they might; and

- **Exploring, through pilots, the effectiveness of social pedagogy in residential care.** This will build on the experiences of successful residential units currently employing social pedagogues from European countries.

Delivering a first class education

11. A high quality education provides the foundation for transforming the lives of children in care. Those who do well in education are more likely to go on to employment, to lead healthier lives and to play a more active part in society. The Government has made a good education for every child in care a priority, including in school admissions policy. However, we need to do more.

To ensure that children in care receive a high quality education we are:

- **Introducing an expectation that local authorities will arrange appropriate high quality early years provision for children in care under five;**

- **Giving children in care the highest priority in school admission arrangements**, including a local authority power to direct schools to admit children in care even if the school is already fully subscribed;

- Reducing disruption to the education of children and young people in care by **introducing a new requirement that the local authority must ensure that the effect of care planning decisions is not to disrupt a child's education and that they must not move schools in years 10 or 11 except in exceptional circumstances**;

- Ensuring a focus in schools on the progression of children in care by **putting the role of the designated teacher on a statutory footing** and supporting this through training and statutory guidance on their role and responsibilities;

- **Personalising the learning of children in care, including providing £500 a year for each child in care at risk of not reaching the expected standards** of achievement, to support their education and development needs and **increasing the availability of one to one tutoring**;

- **Improving support for reducing school absence and exclusion**, including asking all schools and local authorities to put in place strategies to improve the attendance and reduce the need for exclusions of children in care, and reinforcing the principle that exclusion should be an absolute last resort; and

- **Piloting the role of the virtual school head in 11 local authorities.** Virtual school heads will oversee the education of children in care in their authority, and those children in the authority's care who are placed out of authority, as if they were the head of a single school.

Promoting health and wellbeing

12. Good health is vital to the lives of children and young people. It enables them to lead enjoyable and fulfilling lives and underpins achievement at school and in adult life. The task of improving health should be approached holistically – it is not the concern of the NHS alone. Factors such as secure attachment, friendship and engagement in positive leisure activities also promote health and wider wellbeing. We are:

- **Sharpening the focus placed on the needs of children in care by local health partners** through inclusion in the new joint strategic needs assessment, which underpins health service commissioning, and issuing statutory guidance on the health of children in care to local authorities and healthcare bodies;

- **Setting new standards for the support provided to pregnant young women and mothers in care and leaving care and, subject to the Comprehensive Spending Review, introducing named health professionals for all children in care;**

- **Ensuring that the individuals in day to day contact with children and young people in care are better able to provide sex and relationship education;**

- **Considering introducing a new indicator on the emotional and behavioural difficulties of children in care within the new local authority performance management framework;**

- **Transforming the availability of positive activities for children and young people in care**, including free part time access to extended activities, free music tuition in schools and priority status for children in care within local authority youth work;

- **Introducing an expectation that local authorities will make their own leisure provision free for children and young people in care.** This is consistent with the role of the corporate parent;

- **Ensuring that leisure activities form a key part of care planning** and that children and young people are well supported in getting involved in these activities; and

- **Placing a new responsibility on the Director of Children's Services to ensure that children and young people in care participate equally in positive activities along with their peers.**

Transition to adulthood

13. Young people in care often have a difficult move to adulthood. The opportunity to delay the change until they are ready is not always open to them, leading to unwanted transitions that happen too fast. At present, there is an expectation that young people leaving the care system will have the skills necessary to cope on their own. However, young people without parental and family support are often exposed to greater risks than other adolescents. To improve the transition to adulthood we are:

- **Preventing local authorities from discharging young people prematurely from their care placements until they are properly prepared and ready to move on to the next stage of their lives.** This will ensure young people's wishes and feelings are respected and that they are fully involved in decisions that affect them. Moves should only take place if young people are properly prepared;

- **Extending the entitlement to the support of a personal advisor up to the age of 25 for all care leavers** who are either in education or wish to return to education;

- **Piloting ways to enable young people to remain with foster carers up to the age of 21,** providing greater stability for young people more in line with that of their peers;

- **Introducing a national bursary of a minimum of £2,000 for all young people in care who go on to higher education; and**

- **Expecting local authorities to consider, when developing their pledge to children in care, what employment opportunities with training they and their partners can offer young people.**

The role of the practitioner

14. The day to day experience of the corporate parent is embodied for children in care by the work of practitioners. Reforms to services for children in care depend on having a highly skilled, committed and stable workforce that delivers individualised support to children and young people. Children and young people want more stability and they want social workers to listen to them and have more time for them. More needs to be done to tackle recruitment and retention of social workers, and to ensure that they are adequately trained. To improve the role of the practitioner we are:

- **Working with the Children's Workforce Development Council and the General Social Care**

Council on remodelling the social care workforce, to enable social workers to spend more time with the child;

- **Improving the skills and training of social workers** to ensure that they have sufficient understanding of child development and to set their role in the context of the children's services reforms initiated by Every Child Matters;

- **Developing, with partners, tailored recruitment campaigns** which emphasise the particular benefits of working in a children's services environment;

- **Introducing a "Newly Qualified Social Worker" status** that would give a guarantee of support, training and induction to child and family social workers;

- **Piloting 'Social Work Practices' to test whether partnership with external agencies can improve the child's experience of care** and empower the local authority to exercise their corporate parenting function more effectively;

- **Strengthening the role of the Independent Reviewing Officer** to ensure that they provide a more effective check on care planning on behalf of the child, including giving them greater independence; and

- **Ensuring that all children in care who need and want them have access to independent visitors,** and, when making a complaint, to independent advocates.

Next steps

15. We have articulated a clear and bold vision for all children in care. During the consultation on the *Care Matters* Green Paper we worked hard to engage as many individuals and groups as possible to build the case for new and sustained action. We now need to harness the enthusiasm for change and deliver a reform programme that will benefit today's children and young people in care and also have lasting impact for the future care population. To implement the changes set out in this White Paper effectively we will:

- **Seek the earliest opportunity to introduce the right legislative and regulatory framework**, including bringing statutory guidance and relevant National Minimum Standards into line with the changes in this White Paper. Government has a critical role to play in putting in place the right statutory framework for the care system. The revised framework should enable children and young people to receive high quality care and support, and drive improvements in services. In doing so it should set clear expectations while also giving local authorities and their partners as much flexibility as possible to respond to local needs and circumstances;

- **Provide further resources to implement the necessary changes.** We will provide an extra £13.5 million in 2007-08 and £89/£96/£107 million over the 2008-11 Comprehensive Spending Review period of which £22.5m has been set aside for a dedicated change fund. Government Offices (GOs) will provide support for local authorities in the effective implementation of this White Paper;

- **Introduce a new partnership model of delivery.** The responsibility we share for achieving these ambitions means there must be a joint vision for change. We will construct a partnership approach to implementation across the statutory and voluntary sectors; and

- **Work with the private sector.** The private sector has much to offer children in care. Many major companies already do valuable work –increasing young people's access to structured leisure activities and the world of work. We will facilitate a long-term dialogue between private companies and the care system, exploring the potential for building major sponsorship programmes which increase opportunities for children in care across the board.

Chapter 1
Corporate parenting: getting it right

"I believe people in power should listen to young people in care because they never will have gone through half of what we have. They need to understand so that they can do more."

Young person

Summary

Children in care deserve excellent parenting – nurturing, supportive and ambitious care which provides stability, promotes resilience and respects their cultural heritage. Because of their unique relationship with the state, this task is complex and requires careful implementation at each level of the system. This chapter sets out our proposals to support local authorities and their partners in their corporate parenting role by:

- **Expecting every local area to develop a pledge for the children in their care and a children in care council to ensure that children's views can be put directly to those responsible for corporate parenting;**

- **Disseminating new corporate parenting training materials, to help authorities ensure that effective arrangements are in place locally;**

- **Identifying and spreading good practice in corporate parenting through the next round of the Beacon Council Scheme;**

- **Issuing revised National Minimum Standards and consolidated updated statutory guidance on the Children Act 1989 to reflect the vision and requirements of this White Paper; and**

- **Ofsted leading a programme of inspection of services for children in care.**

Introduction

1.1 Children in care[1] deserve the best experiences in life, from excellent parenting and education to a wide range of opportunities to develop their talents and skills, in order to have an enjoyable childhood and successful adult life. Stable placements, emotional wellbeing and support for transitions are essential elements of this success but children and young people will only achieve their potential through the ambition and high expectation of all those involved in their lives.

1.2 This White Paper sets out how, working in partnership with local agencies, we will deliver this vision for success and improve the lives of children in care. It builds on the Green Paper *Care Matters: Transforming the Lives of Children and Young People in Care*[2] published for consultation in October 2006. It is informed by consultation responses, both from adults and from children and young people themselves, and addresses the gaps identified in these responses and the recommendations of the four working groups established following the publication of the *Care Matters* Green Paper.

The case for change

1.3 First and foremost, children in care are children. They have the same needs as any child – for a loving, supportive home life which nurtures and encourages them; for the chance to have fun with their friends and to enjoy and achieve at school. But they also face particular challenges and many of them have specific difficulties that they need extra help and support to deal with.

1.4 The *Care Matters* Green Paper set out the scale of the challenge and the case for change, outlining a range of proposals to improve outcomes for children in care. This White Paper does not therefore restate the scale of the challenge, or the reasons why change is necessary. A summary of responses to the consultation, including a separate summary of responses from children and young people, was published in April[3] 2007. Respondents welcomed the emphasis that the Government was placing on improving the lives of children in care and there was widespread support for the package of proposals put forward.

1.5 We also established four independent working groups to look into best practice in supporting children in care and to explore in more detail some of the ideas floated in the Green Paper. These were:

- **The Future of the Care Population**, chaired by Martin Narey, which explored what our long term vision for the care system should be;

---

1 This White Paper uses the term 'children in care' to include all children being looked after by a local authority, including those subject to care orders under section 31 of the Children Act 1989 and those looked after on a voluntary basis through an agreement with their parents under section 20 of the Children Act 1989

2 http://www.dfes.gov.uk/consultations/downloadableDocs/6731-DfES-Care%20Matters.pdf

3 http://www.dfes.gov.uk/consultations/downloadableDocs/Care%20Matters%20Response.pdf

- **Social Care Practices**, chaired by Professor Julian Le Grand, which investigated the feasibility of piloting social work practices;

- **Better Placements for Children in Care**, chaired by Lord Laming, which looked at how best to secure a positive and sustained placement experience for every child in care; and

- **Best Practice in Schools**, chaired by Dame Pat Collarbone, which identified and put forward suggestions for disseminating good models of supporting the education of children in care.

1.6 The reports of these working groups are published alongside this White Paper and the chapters which follow present the Government's response to their recommendations.

The role of children's services

1.7 Central and local government, service providers, individual professionals and carers[4] are in a vital position of responsibility with regard to children in care. As corporate parents, we must work together to provide everything that a good parent would. As with any parent, this is where the responsibility and accountability for the child's wellbeing and future prospects ultimately lie. We must seek and give due weight to their wishes and feelings. We must champion the needs of children in care and strive to deliver the best for them. We must build children's resilience through helping them to develop secure, stable attachments to their carers, who must have high aspirations for them and deliver high quality care which meets their needs.

1.8 Through the Every Child Matters (ECM) programme, we are reforming children's services to ensure that every child and young person is able to:

- Be healthy

- Stay safe

- Enjoy and achieve

- Make a positive contribution; and

- Achieve economic wellbeing

1.9 In each local area, children's trusts are bringing together services for children, particularly education, children's social care and health. Local authorities have the key responsibility for bringing these partners together, but children's trusts are a multi-agency endeavour. Based on the principles of prevention and early intervention, progressive universalism – giving most help to those in greatest need – and better support for families, services are being delivered in new ways. Sure Start Children's Centres, extended schools and integrated youth services are delivering joined up support based around the needs of children, young people and families. Established services are working in new ways through multi-agency teams, developing common skills, processes

---

4 For the purposes of this White Paper the term 'carer' is used to denote a foster carer or a residential care worker as primary carer.

and language to ensure that they best meet the needs of children and young people and that services are tailored more effectively.

1.10 Accountability has been improved through the appointment of Directors of Children's Services and elected Lead Members for Children's Services, providing a single line of accountability. They are responsible for ensuring that service planning and delivery is coordinated and information is shared across all the relevant partners so that children, young people and their families are supported at the earliest opportunity. This is a significant agenda for change which local partners are embracing energetically, with some exciting innovation happening across the country. It is important to recognise that the work to improve outcomes for children in care is part of this wider reform agenda.

The corporate parenting task

1.11 These reforms provide a strong base from which to pursue an ambitious agenda for children in care. There is some existing excellent practice on which to build. There are many committed and passionate people involved in supporting children in care, and many individual success stories. However, despite the progress made, outcomes for children in care are far from good enough and the gap in outcomes between them and their peers has not narrowed. Children who are in care have a unique relationship with the services that are there to support them. Either because the state is looking after them with the agreement of the child's parents, or – more commonly – because they have been taken into care through a court process having suffered significant harm at home, the local authority is fulfilling some or all of the parenting task.

1.12 For all children, the complicated role of parenting happens on many levels – from basic decisions about their day to day care and the quality of the emotional support they receive, through to big decisions about where a child will live and what school they attend as well as imparting values which help to shape their future aspirations and ambitions.

1.13 For most children, these different levels are fulfilled by the same people but it is more complex for children in care. And children and young people in care themselves have told us repeatedly that they want and need stability and continuity of care so that those who look after them do not change so frequently. The challenge, therefore, is to ensure that the quality of care which children experience meets their need for a secure attachment and promotes their resilience and that this is achieved as far as possible without the need for a series of placements before finding the right one.

Secure attachment

1.14 Secure attachment is essential to the healthy development of children. Babies and children need a secure emotional relationship with one or two main carers, usually a parent, in order to develop physically, emotionally and intellectually. They need to feel safe, protected and nurtured by carers who respond appropriately to them so that they can gradually make sense of the world around them. This secure relationship, or 'attachment', with consistent carers is essential to their development and to learning to trust their carers to meet their needs.

1.15 However, all children in care, including those only in care for a short period of time and those who remain at long term risk of entering care have experienced adversity which impacts on their development. Children in care have often had difficult experiences within their birth families and may have had more than one set of carers since coming into care. They may not have experienced the close, loving relationships that enable children to feel secure and to grow and develop. They may have developed challenging behaviour as a result of this and may find it hard to trust the carers and adults around them.

1.16 Attachment difficulties can happen where the care is not good enough and the carer is not meeting the needs of the child. For some children this may start at birth or soon after; for others it may occur repeatedly throughout their childhood years. Babies' and children's early experiences are now known to affect their brain development. The baby's sensory experience helps to build the growing brain, but neglect,

injury and loss can disrupt this and lead to developmental problems and delay. Insecure attachment with the child's care giver can prevent the child from learning to form close responsive bonds with other people.

1.17 Children in care can be helped to develop more secure attachments with their carers, but carers often need ongoing support and encouragement as it can be a complex and difficult process. Children with insecure attachments frequently show behaviour that repeatedly challenges their relationship with carers, which can be their way of testing the carer's commitment to them.

1.18 It is essential that professionals involved in supporting children and carers have a strong understanding of attachment and of the importance of core practice such as life story work (where a child is helped to make sense of their past experiences) so that they may help an abused, harmed or neglected child to develop a secure emotional base. It is also important that children, carers and professionals have access to appropriate therapeutic interventions that can address the damage caused by previous experiences to a child's ability to form attachments.

Resilience

1.19 It is through secure attachments and positive experiences that children and young people develop the resilience that they need in life. Resilience refers to an individual's capacity to adapt successfully to change and to stressful events in healthy and constructive ways.

It involves an interaction between both risk and protective processes that act to modify the effects of an adverse life event. The factors associated with behavioural resilience in children and young people are outlined in Box 1.1.

Role of the corporate parent – making the system work

1.20 Respondents to our consultation told us that improving the role of the corporate parent is key to the successful implementation of *Care Matters*. It is about more than providing food and shelter: a good corporate parent must offer everything that a good parent would provide and more, addressing both the difficulties which the children experience and the challenges of parenting within a complex system of different services. This means that children in care should be cared about, not just cared for and that all aspects of their development should be nurtured requiring a 'corporate' approach across

Box 1.1: Resilience Factors[5]

Individual characteristics

Learning and problem solving skills (intelligence)

Self-regulation skills (self control)

Feeling positive about oneself and our capabilities (self worth)

Positive outlook on life (hopefulness)

Appealing qualities (talents, skills, able to engage)

Relationships and parenting

Strong connections with one or more effective parents

Parenting quality (providing affection, monitoring, expectations, setting boundaries)

Bonds with other positive adults (family and friends, mentors, teachers)

Connections to positive and competent peers

Community context

Effective schools

Opportunities to develop skills and talents

Quality of the community (safety, positive organization)

Connections to positive organizations (clubs, faith groups)

Socioeconomic advantages

---

5   Masten, A.S. (2001). Ordinary Magic: Resilience Processes in Development. *American Psychologist*, 56, 227-238

all of the agencies involved in the children's trust, with a clear line of accountability for delivery.

1.21 There are various levels at which the parenting function for children in care needs to operate in order to ensure that they receive the sort of good parenting that we would expect for any child – from the day to day care provided by foster carers or residential care workers, to the decisions taken by social workers, right up to the strategic level of the Director of Children's Services and their partners in the children's trust. It is important that children have a chance to shape and influence the parenting that they receive at every level – from expressing their wishes and feelings about the individual care they receive in their placements, through to helping to shape the overall strategy for children in their area through a Children in Care Council (see Box 1.2).

1.22 Responsibility for providing excellent corporate parenting must be shared across all services for children, and at all levels. But is it also important to have clear accountability for improving service delivery and outcomes for children and young people in care. The Director of Children's Services and the Lead Member for Children's Services are, therefore, pivotal to ensuring that all services are operating in a way that supports the best possible outcomes for

each child in their care. In addition to local authority services, other agencies share in these responsibilities as public sector services providing support to children in the care of the State. Section 10 of the Children Act 2004 names those agencies (including health, the police and all tiers of local government) which have a duty to co-operate to secure the welfare of children and this duty underpins the arrangements for effective corporate parenting.

Improving corporate parenting

1.23 Box 1.2 summarises the systems and processes that need to be in place to help a local authority meet its responsibilities as a corporate parent. Corporate parenting may be delivered through different systems and structures in different authorities. However, in all cases children and young people in care should be given a strong voice, including those most at risk of marginalisation, such as disabled children and those with communication difficulties. Directors of Children's Services and Lead Members should take the lead in ensuring that they are listened to – both individually and collectively – and that their needs are met. In each area the components outlined below should be in place, irrespective of the local corporate parenting structure.

Box 1.2: Components of effective corporate parenting

Whatever structures exist in a children's services authority, there are certain key elements of corporate parenting that need to be in place.

The Director of Children's Services and Lead Member have overall responsibility for leading corporate parenting arrangements – both across the authority and with its partners in the children's trust.

Authorities may also appoint a group of senior officials with responsibility for the corporate parenting of children in care. The **accountability** and **governance** arrangements of these groups must be clear.

Whatever structures exist in a children's services authority, **children's participation** is an essential part of the process. We expect every local authority to establish a *Children in Care Council* to ensure that every child has the opportunity to air their views. In making these arrangements, the local authority should consider in particular the needs of disabled children and very young children, and of those children who are not members of the council themselves.

Through the *Children in Care Council*, children and young people should be able to put their experiences of the care system **directly to those responsible for corporate parenting** including the DCS and Lead Member, who should demonstrate how they will maintain contact with children and young people in care.

In exercising their functions, those responsible for coordinating corporate parenting need effective **management information**. This information should cover:

- quantitative data, such as education and health outcomes for looked after children, and

- qualitative data, such as the views of consumers of services concerning the quality and suitability of the services to meet their needs and achieve good outcomes

Strategic planning, policies, protocols and partnerships should assist and inform the work of the group. Children's trust arrangements, underpinned by the 'duty to cooperate' (Children Act 2004) and the schools' duty to promote wellbeing, provide the context for developing better corporate parenting. Children and Young People's Plans should set out how the children's trust will address the needs of looked after children and care-leavers. Transition to adult services, as well as the provision of adult services for parents and carers, should be incorporated within this strategic plan to ensure coordinated services that meet the assessed needs of the child.

1.24 Strong corporate parenting arrangements are central to improving all services for children and young people in care. To strengthen the focus on corporate parenting at the strategic level within local authorities and their partner agencies, we will:

- **Introduce an Annual Stocktake** – a national Ministerial event to review progress in improving outcomes for children in care, with key stakeholders and representatives of local government, health and young people in care;

- **Disseminate new Government-funded comprehensive corporate parenting training materials**, developed by the National Children's Bureau, to help authorities to ensure that effective arrangements are in place locally;

- **Through the next round of the Beacon Council Scheme**, identify and spread good practice in corporate parenting; and

- **Monitor local authorities' arrangements for ensuring that young people contribute meaningfully to service planning** within the children's trust through Children in Care Councils or other structures.

1.25 We expect **every local area to develop a pledge** for the children in their care.

The pledges should be developed locally through the children's trust arrangements and may include a regional dimension. They should ensure that:

- Children in care are aware of the basic statutory requirements with which local authorities should already be complying;

- Children are aware of the key opportunities and benefits offered to them locally;

- Children in care are supported to engage with positive activities as much as possible, for example, the cadets, scouts or guides and local sports clubs, including support for their own hobbies and interests;

- Children in care have been consulted and involved in developing the pledge, including those with special needs and disabled children; and

- The pledge is regularly reviewed and reflected in the local Children and Young People's Plan or equivalent.

Basic elements of the care pledge:

- A commitment to involve children in decisions which affect them and to take account of their wishes and expressed feelings about the services they receive.

- Qualified social workers for every child in care with clear arrangements in place for the child in care to contact his/her social worker as necessary

- Effective assessment of individual needs and an up to date care plan based on those needs

- A placement with carers who can meet needs

- Contact with siblings and birth parents in line with their care plan

- Regular reviews in which children will be enabled to participate meaningfully (particularly for disabled children with communication difficulties)

- Services which recognise the diverse ethnic and cultural needs of the children

- Access to advocacy services if children have a complaint

- An Independent Reviewing Officer to ensure children's rights are upheld

- Access to high quality free early years provision at age 3 and 4

- A place at a good school

- A designated teacher in school to ensure high quality support in school

- Details of support available to participate in positive leisure time activities

- Support to reduce absence from school

- Help to catch up with school work if they fall behind

- Regular assessments of their health (physical and emotional)

- Details of support available when they move on from care

- The support young people can expect when entering further and higher education

- How the local authority will support young people seeking employment, including employment with training.

Young London Matters – Care Pledge

Young London Matters (YLM) is a partnership approach to Every Child Matters (ECM) in London which aims to improve outcomes for London's most vulnerable children and young people.

YLM is developing a pan-London pledge for children in care based around the five ECM outcomes and a core entitlement to which appropriate pan-London agencies and local areas will sign up. The engagement of young people and finding out what is important to them within a pledge is key to the process. Individual boroughs will be able to adapt the pan-London pledge to reflect the particular circumstances and the views of children in care and care leavers in their area.

A number of consultation events will take place during the summer and early autumn in 2007, involving young people and key stakeholder organisations, giving young people the opportunity to put their views across to pan-London organisations who can help turn their views into a reality.

Following the events, a draft pledge will be prepared and consulted on more widely. The aim is for the pan-London pledge to have been adopted by boroughs and other stakeholders by the end of March 2008.

The Lead Member for Children's Services

1.26 All elected Members of a local authority have a critical role in both setting the strategic direction of a Council's services and in determining policy priorities for the local community. As such, they have it in their power to affect the lives of the children in their community for the better. This duty and power has the greatest significance for children in their care given that the Council as a whole has the role and responsibility of acting as corporate parent.

1.27 The Lead Member for Children's Services has statutory responsibility for ensuring that the Council discharges its duties to children and families effectively and that key partners co-operate in this delivery. The new provisions in the Local Government and Public Involvement in Health Bill are intended to strengthen the role of Councillors generally to scrutinise the delivery of health services within the local area (see Chapter 6).

1.28 Given the breadth of Lead Member responsibility, it may be appropriate that the Corporate Parenting responsibilities are shared by another Councillor designated for this role. Whatever the supporting arrangements for Lead Members, it is critical that the designated Member has the experience, time and political authority to carry out this role effectively and that ultimate political accountability remains with the statutory Lead Member for Children's Services.

Getting the basics right – improving assessment and care planning in a permanence framework

1.29 As well as these reforms at the strategic level, it is equally important to ensure good quality and consistent individual needs assessment, care planning and service provision for each individual child. Subsequent chapters of this White Paper set out how we will improve support for family and friends carers, and improve the services provided by social workers, schools, youth services and health. But for children in care, all of this support must be grounded in a high quality assessment of their needs and a care plan which is based on those needs.

1.30 More effective care planning will ensure that as many children as possible have the chance to experience a loving family and strong connections to adults who have a long term commitment to them. This framework of emotional, physical and legal conditions gives a child a sense of security, continuity and identity; it gives them 'permanence'. Every child in care should have a plan for permanence by the time of their second review – four months from coming into care. The plan should identify tasks and timescales for ensuring that this permanence plan is achieved and delivery will be monitored through the statutory review process.

1.31 The resilience factors set out in Box 1.1 at the start of this chapter provide a framework for considering provision for children in care, focusing on the quality of their day to day experience. The three domains set out in box 1.1 map on to those used in the Framework for the Assessment of Children in Need and their Families which in turn provides the conceptual model for the Integrated Children's System, used for the assessment, planning, intervention and review of all children in need.

1.32 It is essential that front line practitioners understand the theoretical underpinning to their work, and that the core functions of assessing need, planning and intervening and reviewing the impact of those interventions are carried out consistently. We will **strengthen the focus on these core functions by:**

- **Bringing together all the requirements for care planning in one set of regulations and issuing accompanying statutory guidance as part of the revised Children Act 1989 guidance. This will be issued in 2009;**

- **Completing the full implementation of the Integrated Children's System in every local authority;**

- **Strengthening the independence of Independent Reviewing Officers; and**

- **Exploring the implications of these changes for social workers' training.**

Barnet's five year financial strategy – spending up front in order to achieve longer term savings

The number of children looked after by Barnet was increasing at a rate of 11% per year from the late 1990s until 2002/03. This resulted in large overspends, children moving too slowly through the system and overall unsatisfactory service delivery. Difficulties were compounded by poor social work recruitment and retention. 60% of Barnet's children in care were placed in the independent sector.

Barnet developed a "Five-year Invest to Save Strategy" to reduce the numbers of children in the care system and improve recruitment and retention and service delivery. In 2003/04 the strategy was approved by Cabinet who increased the base budget by £5.5 million, to be repaid by 2007/08 through an annual reduction in the placement budget. The service was restructured to increase the focus on safely preventing children from coming into care and to strengthen commissioning and performance management. An innovative strategy for the recruitment and retention of staff and foster carers was developed.

Four years later the number of children in care has decreased by 18% and social work vacancies have reduced leading to improved service delivery. There is enhanced placement choice and the number of children placed outside Barnet has now reduced. Managers have confidence that staff vacancies and placement costs are manageable and controllable. Outcomes for Barnet's children in care continue to improve.

Delivering better value for money

1.33 Spending on services for children and young people in care has increased substantially, even whilst the numbers in care have levelled off. It represents a significant proportion of the funding for children's services – nearly £2bn a year is spent by local authorities in England just on placements for children in care – and yet outcomes are still unacceptably low. The system does not yet do enough to address the harm that children have suffered before entering care.

1.34 Since 2004-05, local authorities have made significant inroads in delivering better value to enable resources to be used to improve outcomes for children and young people. For children's services alone, local authorities have exceeded their 2.5% efficiency target through a range of innovative and incremental changes to the way services are commissioned and delivered, and the way the workforce is deployed. Many of these improvements have been in the way they deliver services for children in care, care leavers and children on the edge of care.

1.35 Local authorities must build on and extend this good practice if they are to meet the Government's target of delivering efficiency gains of 3% per annum from 2008-09.

1.36 The reforms set out in this White Paper play a crucial role in supporting local authorities to deliver better value for money over the Comprehensive

Spending Review period of 2008-2011. In particular, the reforms will aim to improve:

- early identification and support to enable more children who are at risk of going into care to remain in their families;

- the recruitment and retention issues in some regions and ensuring social work teams work more effectively together;

- the way that needs are assessed and services designed to meet those needs;

- the commissioning process, including piloting approaches to regional commissioning; and

- the use of more evidence-based interventions for the most challenging children and those with complex needs, who too often end up in extremely costly provision which does not meet their needs.

1.37 These reforms therefore have a significant contribution to make to the efficiency gains that local authorities are required to deliver. Much of the answer is not about new resources, but we recognise that turning this situation around will require some investment, and that service provision varies significantly across different areas of the country.

1.38 In order to build further capacity to implement the changes in this White Paper we will **provide additional resources of £13.5m in 2007-08 and £89/96/107million over the 2008-11**

comprehensive spending review period.

1.39 As part of this funding, we will **make available a change fund in 2007-08 for local authorities who have audited their systems for supporting children in care and those on the edge of care and identified their priorities for improvement**. Support will be offered for innovative proposals that are evidence-based and clearly linked to improved outcomes for children and young people.

1.40 Good corporate parenting requires local agencies to take a longer term view on local budgets if change is to be embedded – particularly if services are to be focused on earlier intervention and prevention. Too often, decisions are made based on short term funding pressures, which will ultimately prove to be more costly. As the case study above shows, a three to five year strategy can help deliver improved cost-effectiveness and underpin long-term shifts in priorities – for example, enabling a better approach to early intervention and prevention, whilst still meeting the needs of those who are in care.

Inspection, standards and guidance

1.41 Strong accountability is a vital part of improving the role of the corporate parent and ensuring that all partners in the children's trust contribute to improving outcomes for children in care.

1.42 The 2006 Local Government White Paper, *Strong and Prosperous Communities*, set out radical proposals for new-style Local Area Agreements (LAAs), which will become the key "delivery contract" between central and local government. From 2008, LAAs will be the single mechanism through which central Government will agree targets with local authorities and their partners on outcomes delivered by local government on its own or in partnership.

1.43 The Government is considering how best to reflect national priorities for local authorities, working alone or in partnership with other services, in the set of approximately 200 national indicators from which all these targets will derive. Each area will agree up to 35 targets for improvement, as well as the statutory education and early years targets which DfES already specifies. Our ambition is that the new national indicator set, from which the LAA targets are negotiated, will include a strong focus on children in care, including statutory targets on the education of children in care.

1.44 Inspection of services is essential to ensure that services are fairly scrutinised and outcomes are improved. By March 2007, 78 local authorities had received a Joint Area Review (JAR) of their services for children and young people. This multi-inspectorate process assesses how well services across the children's trust are improving outcomes for children, young people and their families. The remaining 72 authorities will have their JAR by September 2008. These remaining JARs will be focused rather than assessing all services, but will judge how services are contributing to improving outcomes for children in care.

1.45 Following the completion of the current programme of JARs, inspectorates will move to a model of proportionate, risk-based inspection of local authorities, following an annual risk assessment led by the Audit Commission. Because of the particular needs of children in care, **Ofsted will lead a programme of inspection of services for children in care**.

1.46 At an individual service level, inspection looks at the quality of services for children in care. Fostering services and children's homes are subject to regulatory inspection to ensure that they are complying with National Minimum Standards (NMS). We are currently reviewing the National Minimum Standards for fostering services, children's homes and adoption and will **issue revised NMS in 2009** which reflect the vision and requirements of this White Paper. These minimum standards underpin all regulatory inspections by Ofsted of fostering services and children's homes (see Chapter 3).

1.47 To support local authorities in improving their corporate parenting we will **issue a revised version of the existing Children Act 1989 Statutory Guidance**. Through this comprehensive consolidated and updated set of guidance, we will set out in one place the full range of policy and practice requirements for all local authorities to deliver their statutory responsibilities for children in care, including those proposed in this White Paper. All the references in this White Paper to statutory Children Act 1989 guidance relate to this revised guidance.

1.48 Finally, we will work with Government Offices to ensure a continued focus on the needs of children in care throughout their work with local areas. There will be a particular focus on supporting the developments set out in this White Paper, and on examining the overall approach to care, exploring issues around consistency and variation across regions, and sharing best practice.

Chapter 2
Family and parenting support

"Families should be supported to stay together when to do so would be in the best interests of the child. Where this is not the case then care should be used as a positive option and not as a substitute for lack of proper support."

A National Voice

Summary

A key element of the *Care Matters* Green Paper, reinforced by the strength of consultation responses, was the need to support children at home with their families where possible. The Future of the Care Population Working Group also made firm recommendations in this area and this chapter sets out how we will refocus services in order to ensure that where it is in children's best interests, they are enabled and supported to live at home. Our strategy includes:

- **Encouraging local authorities to analyse and manage their care populations more proactively;**

- **Improved parenting support;**

- **Pilots for new family-based interventions for older children and young people;**

- **Improvements to the arrangements for short break care;**

- **A new framework for enabling children to live with their wider family or friends; and**

- **Wider developments which will support the early intervention/prevention agenda.**

Introduction

2.1   In response to the *Care Matters* Green Paper, many children and young people told us that they would prefer to remain with their birth parents or wider family rather than come into care and that they wanted services to facilitate this wherever possible. Children and young people consulted by the Children's Rights Director stated that care by a relative should be considered in all cases before any decision is made that a child should come into care. It is essential that services are designed to identify early those families who need support, including children in need of safeguarding, in order to prevent the need for children to enter care.

2.2 This approach, however, needs to be a sophisticated one, with a range of services made available to support families as and when they need it. These will include intensive interventions where family difficulties are complex and enduring; better access to support care and short term breaks; tailored support for adults whose own difficulties are impacting on their ability to parent, and comprehensive packages of support to ensure that children are enabled to return home from care in a planned and sustainable way.

Managing the care population

2.3 One of the questions posed by the *Care Matters* Green Paper was whether or not the Government ought to seek deliberately to manage the size of the care population. The suggestion was put forward that such a strategy might have as its ultimate goal a smaller care population, with more children being enabled to be supported at home.

2.4 The Future of the Care Population Working Group considered this question in detail and its report, published alongside this White Paper, came to some interesting conclusions. The group felt strongly that while a smaller care population could well indicate a successful children's services system managing to keep more

children safely at home with their families, it may not always be an indicator of effective safeguarding practice. In particular, children and young people themselves expressed a strong concern that such a strategy could lead to some children and young people being left at home in dangerous situations when care would actually be the best place for them. Indeed some thought they should perhaps come into care more quickly.

2.5 On the basis of the analysis set out in the working group's report, the Government is persuaded that to set a numerical target at this stage for the size of the care population would entail unavoidable risk. However, the working group concluded that there was merit in continuing to examine these questions. Some local authorities have managed to reduce the numbers of children in their care through an explicit decision to do so, and where such a strategy is coupled with comprehensive family support and intervention arrangements, the working group felt that it could be to the benefit of all vulnerable children in the area.

2.6 The working group was also struck by the significant differences in the numbers of children in care between similar authorities, suggesting that there are some inconsistencies in practice. A child with particular needs and family circumstances in one area would be in care while in another area the same child would be supported at home.

2.7 There is thus something of a 'postcode lottery' in care and it is important that local authorities proactively monitor their care populations in order to ensure that care is provided only for those children for whom it is assessed as the best option. The implementation of the Integrated Children's System (ICS) enables local authorities to aggregate information about individual children and their needs in order to profile their population of children in care as well as those supported at home. We will therefore:

- **Ask Government Offices to work with local authorities to establish the reasons behind differential rates of care, with a particular focus on:**

  - **The thresholds used for bringing children into care; and**

  - **The decision-making mechanisms for accommodating a child with the parents' agreement or applying to the courts for a care order.**

2.8 This work will be linked to the current benchmarking arrangements and this analysis will be looked at in the first Annual Stocktake on the care system to consider the implications of these differences.

Strong attachments

2.9 Children and young people repeatedly emphasised during consultation that links with family and friends are very important to them and it is vital that, in implementing the *Care Matters* reforms, local authorities help to facilitate these relationships whether or not a child is in care. These relationships provide important continuity where placements may be unstable and can also provide emotional and practical support during the transition to adulthood. Many children stay in care for only a short time and then return to vulnerable families where support and services continue to be needed. For younger children, children's centres can offer important support and continuity during a time of transition between birth family and foster home.

2.10 Contact while in care is something which children have raised frequently. They want to have more contact with people who are important to them and help to manage what can sometimes be a difficult experience. The arrangements for contact must be at the heart of care planning, including in

Resilience in children grows out of a strong sense of belonging, out of good self esteem and out of a sense of efficacy or being able to achieve things and make a difference. Fundamentally these qualities grow out of supportive relationships with parents, relatives, teachers or other adults (or sometimes peers) who offer in-depth commitment, encouragement and support.

Gilligan 2001[1]

---

1 Gilligan, R. (2001) Promoting Resilience – A resource guide on working with children in the care system, BAAF

those processes and procedures related to adoption. It is therefore important that, other than where this is clearly not in the child's best interest, local authorities treat birth families as important partners in the care planning process in line with statutory requirements.

2.11 Family Group Conferencing, which can engage the support of wider family and friends at an early stage of concerns about a child, to support birth parents and reduce the need for the child to enter care, is a particularly good way of ensuring that all of the resources within the family's wider social networks have been tapped for the benefit of the child. Following the launch of the Family Group Conference toolkit in November 2006 at a national conference, we will:

- **Fund a programme of regional training events to equip managers and practitioners with the necessary skills to develop and sustain the Family Group Conference model.**

Family and parenting support

2.12 In recent years the Government has placed a renewed focus on the importance of good parenting – in particular through the publication earlier this year of *Every Parent Matters*[2] – and has developed a number of initiatives through which the State can support parents in their role. It is vital that, as the *Care Matters* White Paper is implemented across the country, local authorities and other partners ensure that children in care and those on the edge of care, benefit from these new arrangements. Parents whose children are at risk of coming into care, as well as foster carers and residential care workers, can all benefit from the evidence-based parenting programmes

Family Group Conferencing and Prevention

Clara, aged ten, was referred for an FGC by her education welfare officer due to poor school attendance. Her mother, a lone parent, was suffering from long term depression. The main presenting problem was her inability to encourage Clara to get up and prepare for school. Clara was also distracted during the school day due to her concerns for her mother's wellbeing. The aim of the FGC was to help Clara, her mother, extended family and agencies explore potential sources of support. It was crucial to put this in place at this stage, as Clara was about to transfer to secondary school. The resulting plan from the FGC was increased support for the mother by adult mental health services. A friend of the family agreed to drop by each morning to walk with Clara to school. Clara was to be supported at the new school by a pastoral support worker, and a referral was made to the local young carers support group. A maternal aunt also agreed to increase her support at weekends and monitor the plan. Clara has since settled at her new school and is doing well.

---

2 Every Parent Matters: DfES 2007, www.everychildmatters.gov.uk

which are currently being rolled out across the country.

2.13 It is essential that families who face particular challenges, such as those with disabled children, receive practical support and advice to prevent problems escalating. The Government report *Aiming high for disabled children: better support for families*, published in May 2007, announced additional resources to evaluate good practice on early interventions, such as sleep programmes and behaviour management, to assist practitioners and parents.

2.14 Government guidance[3] has emphasised the need for support to be available to families at the earliest point at which it is needed and to develop a system-wide integrated continuum of support services. These will be available through SureStart Children's Centres and extended schools as well as through more specialist services. Family Intervention Projects aimed at reducing antisocial behaviour are currently available in 50 local authorities. The aim of all parenting support services is to enable parents to exercise their parental responsibilities effectively for their children in a way which safeguards and promotes their welfare.

2.15 In particular, the new Government-funded National Academy for Parenting Practitioners (NAPP) will provide training, development and support for the parenting workforce; support the

training of a range of professionals including social workers and clinical psychologists in evidence-based interventions and act as a national source of advice on research evidence as to what works in parenting support.

2.16 The Future of the Care Population Working Group report emphasised the need for effective family support to enable children to remain at home and there is a significant body of evidence to support the emphasis on early intervention for high risk children and families. A range of effective interventions have been developed to address family problems across the age and need spectrum. Whilst the Webster-Stratton parenting programme is now widely available and has proved both popular and effective with foster carers, as well as with birth families, there is a need for more widespread implementation of a range of approaches that are known to work for families with complex problems where there is a real risk of children coming into care or to enable and support their return home.

2.17 Research studies commissioned as part of the Department of Health Supporting Parents Initiative[4] showed that parents in the general population with lower levels of difficulty wanted services to be accessible, professional, responsive and respectful. However, those parents who are harder to engage are likely to have multiple, overlapping problems, poor relationships with family and friends

3   Parenting Support: Guidance for Local Authorities in England. October 2006 www.everychildmatters.gov.uk

4   Quinton, D. (2004) *Supporting Parents: Messages from Research*, DfES and DH. London

and fragile and violent relationships in the home. Importantly, they are likely to be pessimistic about services and hostile to offers of help. The implications for services are therefore clear – services must be multi-systemic in their approach, able to address the families' difficulties in a number of domains and settings and be extremely well coordinated, balancing the focus on individuals with a focus on the family system.

2.18 The Government has made considerable progress over the last decade in improving outcomes for the majority of families but more needs to be done to improve the outcomes of the minority with highest needs. The Families at Risk Review[5] has been led by the Social Exclusion Unit Task Force. An interim report was published on 18 June which focuses on the small minority – around 2-3% of families – identified in Reaching Out: an Action Plan on Social Exclusion, who experienced multiple and entrenched problems. The review examines modern family life and the complex role of family as a potential source of both risk and resilience. It also considers the way in which services and systems work with the most excluded families to break the cycle of disadvantage. A final report will be published in autumn 2007.

2.19 As a result of new evidence and a better understanding of the importance of health-led early intervention and prevention in pregnancy and the first years of life, the Government is piloting an evidence-based programme to improve the outcomes of the most at risk children and families. The Reaching Out Report recommended the testing of the nurse-led home visiting programme, the Nurse Family Partnership, which has achieved impressive results with over 25 years of testing and development in the US. This programme is now being piloted in 10 NHS and local authority sites across England, where it is delivered by specially trained health visitors and midwives working from Children's Centres as part of universal health services.

Responses to neglect

2.20 Neglect is the most common category of abuse under which children's names are placed on the child protection register. In 2006, 43% of the total number of registrations were due to neglect – and parents of neglected children are often well known to a range of professionals. It is therefore crucial that those working with them are alert to any evidence that a child or children may be being neglected and take such steps as are necessary to safeguard and promote their welfare. We have commissioned five projects which focus on neglect as part of our Safeguarding Children research programme. This programme commenced in 2006; four projects are due for completion by the end of 2008, with the fifth due at the end of 2009. It

---

5   http://www.cabinetoffice.gov.uk/social_exclusion_task_force/index.asp

is anticipated that the findings from these studies will inform improvements to the interventions available and we will:

- **Develop training resources based on the findings from these research projects.**

2.21 These resources will assist professionals to identify neglect and, when working with children and families, to develop and use effective interventions in order to achieve good outcomes for this group of children.

Support for adults with particular difficulties

2.22 The parenting agenda also highlights the need for greater integration across children's and adults' services, supported by the 2006 Government White Paper *Our Health, Our care, Our Say*. Increasing numbers of children are entering care because of the particular needs of their parents and it is vital that adults' services recognise the particular circumstances of clients who are also parents. In particular it is vital that adults and children's services work together to identify and address the needs of young carers who may be at particular risk of social exclusion.

2.23 The particular effects on children of substance misusing parents are well-documented, as is the scale of the problem, which is reflected in high rates of care proceedings in some parts of

the country. The *Hidden Harm*[6] report explored these issues in detail. The needs of the adults who are drug and alcohol misusers are not the prime focus of care proceedings and there can be particular difficulties in aligning timescales for adult treatment with the child's timescale in terms of achieving permanence. In order to provide a court service which is directly linked with adult treatment services and which is more responsive to the needs of children and families in these circumstances, we are therefore:

- **Piloting a Family Drug and Alcohol Court, to begin in January 2008, to evaluate its capacity to improve the engagement of adults in treatment services and increase their capacity to provide stable care for their children.**

2.24 The model, originally developed in the US, will provide intensive assessment, support, interventions (one-to-one and group work) and care plan coordination for families affected by parental substance misuse whose children are in care proceedings. A specialist District Judge will play an important role in encouraging and motivating parents to engage with services through regular court review hearings. Recent findings from the evaluation of the model in the United States show promising improvements in outcomes for both children and adults.

6   Hidden Harm. Responding to the needs of children of problem drug users, Advisory Council on the Misuse of Drugs. June 2003

Interventions for families with older children and young people

2.25 The Future of the Care Population Working Group, while not advocating a deliberate strategy to reduce the population, did nonetheless identify certain groups of children and young people who, with the right support, could most effectively be supported at home. One of these groups was older young people who often come into care as teenagers.

2.26 The working group felt that this was a group of young people who needed particular attention and for whom local authorities would be well advised to commission specific family interventions. We are therefore:

- **Funding the development of Multi-systemic Therapy (MST) as an effective specialist intervention for older children and young people on the edge of care. Pilots will begin in Spring 2008.**

2.27 This intervention combines family and cognitive behavioural therapy strategies with a range of other family support services and tackles factors contributing to a young person's behaviour problems and poor family functioning across settings and systems. We will build on the current experience of developing Multi-systemic Therapy programmes in the UK to test its effectiveness in enabling high risk adolescents with antisocial or offending behaviour and other complex needs to remain at home with their family. The programme will be

fully evaluated in order to assess its relevance for all local areas.

Support care and short term breaks

2.28 Care can also be an effective short term intervention to support families to remain together. It is not just for children who enter the system and remain there long term. There are a number of ways of using care as part of a family support service and it is also important to remember that most children return home from care within a year but may remain vulnerable children once back in the community. Short term breaks such as support care or respite care can therefore play a valuable role in supporting families under stress, as well as providing broader experiences and opportunities for children and young people.

2.29 Support care provides a very flexible resource to support families under stress offering, for example, after school homework support, or weekends away for boys in single parent families to engage in hobbies with a "support care family". It is very much a local community-based model and the two families are usually living in the same neighbourhood. One parent described the support carer as 'someone like me but without the problems'.

2.30 Fostering Network has just completed a Government-funded project to pilot a number of support care schemes. These pilots, following the model first successfully developed in Bradford Social Services Department, have proved to be very effective and popular with users and very cost-effective in enabling children to remain long term in their birth or wider family. The report from the project will be published as a book later in 2007. We will therefore:

- **Encourage all local authorities to commission 'support care' as part of their range of provision for children in need.**

2.31 *Aiming high for disabled children: better support for families* highlighted the importance of short break provision for disabled children and their families. The review, as part of its broader recommendations, announced that we would:

- **Provide £280 million over three years to deliver a step change in provision of short breaks to reduce family stress and ensure**

disabled children are better supported in their families.

2.32 The *Care Matters* Green Paper sought views on whether children who benefit from these short breaks (also known as 'respite care') should be classified as being 'in care', concerns having been raised previously about whether such status is a proportionate response and about variability in practice between different local areas.

2.33 The Government believes that children in short breaks should only be given looked after status where that is in their best interests. 'Looked after' status should not be an automatic response to the use of this provision. For those with complex health needs, overnight provision may be appropriate. However, children should only be placed away from home overnight after the local

---

Sam aged 12 with a diagnosis of ADHD

Bradford pioneered Support Care over ten years ago with the aim of supporting children and young people at home. It helps to prevent family breakdown and children being accommodated, and avoids the need for long term care.

Sam's home placement with his father and grandmother broke down as they struggled with his demanding behaviour. He went to live with his mother, who found herself immediately in difficulties and requested that he be accommodated.

A weekend placement was set up with Support Care. Routines were established by the carer, who quickly engaged with Sam. An in-house training session on ADHD was helpful in her understanding and management of his difficulties.

The carer supported Sam's mother and advised her on how to respond to her son's behavioural difficulties. Sam's mother has become more confident in coping with her son's behaviour, feels less isolated with difficulties, and occasionally contacts the carer for advice.

It has proven to be a highly successful preventative intervention for children and young people on the edge of care and is a valued part of the family support strategy within Bradford Children's Services.

authority has carried out an in-depth assessment of the needs of the child and family, including ascertaining the wishes and feelings of the child. Following the assessment, they should determine whether the child and family should receive services and, if so, which services will be appropriate and the relevant legal status. However, local authorities and families have told us that there is confusion about the legal status of some of these placements and the requirements for assessment which surround these arrangements. To address this we will:

- **Issue statutory guidance (within the revised Children Act 1989 guidance) specifically on the issues of support/short break care to clarify the applicable regulations for different settings and arrangements. The guidance will set out the circumstances in which it would be expected that the child would be looked after.**

New framework for family and friends care

2.34 Family and friends carers play a key role in enabling children to remain with people they know and trust if they cannot live with their parents and these arrangements happen both within and outside the care system. We know that many family and friends carers are often older carers with health and financial difficulties of their own yet they provide a stable, safe and nurturing home during a short term family crisis or until the child reaches adulthood and beyond.

2.35 Our focus here is on three types of placement: those placements with relatives or family friends where a child would otherwise be looked after; those who are already looked after; and those who are returning from a care placement to be cared for by relatives or friends.

2.36 It is essential that carers in these circumstances receive proper support and recognition and we intend to provide this though a new framework for family and friends care which will set out the expectations of an effective service to enable children to remain within their wider family and communities.

2.37 We know that financial and practical support are the highest priority for carers, followed by training and access to Family Group Conferencing (where professionals convene a discussion with the child's wider family and friends about what support they might be able to offer a family in difficulty). These issues were debated in both the Future of the Care Population and Placements Working Groups and it is clear that current arrangements are not sufficiently robust. Concerns which we will address in the new arrangements include:

- Variation across the country in the extent to which family and friends placements are used;

- Absence of policy frameworks to underpin services to these families and, where they are in place, inconsistent application of the policy;

Support for Kinship Care

Kent has a longstanding arrangement with NCH to provide Kinship Care Support through "KISKA" (Kent Independent Support for Kinship and Adoption).

KISKA's Kinship care support includes:

- information and advice on parenting issues;

- help to access information in relation to their rights and services;

- advocacy and support in relation to education, health and housing issues;

- practical advice in relation to contact with the child's birth parents & other family members; and

- help in developing effective support networks within their local community.

KISKA's role in supporting kinship care is embedded within a culture of normalising children's living arrangements and empowering families to identify avenues of support within their own family and friend networks. Kent's Family Group Conferencing service is key to this process.

One of the other services offered by KISKA is independent support for birth relatives where there is an adoption plan in place for a child. Support is offered in various ways such as independent explanation of the adoption process, or accompanying the birth parent to the court hearings. A support group has been established for birth parents whose children have been recently placed for adoption. The experiences of the group will be used to develop leaflets for other birth parents. Knowledge gained by staff from this area of work has informed practice in supporting contact arrangements, and in intermediary services offered to birth relatives and adopted adults.

The KISKA service is currently being evaluated to ensure that it is providing the right support for kinship carers and the children who live with them.

- Lack of transparency of entitlements and services available and inequitable treatment of carers, and

- Suitability of the approval processes for family and friends carers.

2.38 We will put in place a 'gateway approach' to family and friends care to make sure that it is considered as an option at the first and every subsequent stage of decision-making by:

- **Introducing a requirement that relatives and friends are, as far as possible, considered in all cases as potential carers as part of the care plan lodged with the court at the outset of care proceedings.**

2.39 *The Child Care Proceedings System in England and Wales*, published by DCA and DfES in May 2006, recommended that adults with a significant relationship to the child should have access to proposed Level 2 pre-proceedings advice in circumstances where local authorities have informed parents that they plan to apply for a Care Order.

2.40 This will form a key part of the new care planning guidance issued as part of the revised Children Act 1989 guidance, described in Chapter 1. It will start at the point of a core assessment where local authorities should ensure that, when assessing the wider family and environmental factors, consideration is given to the willingness and capacity of the wider family to care for the child on a shorter or longer term basis. The option should also be considered in plans developed as part of care proceedings and as part of any consideration of permanence options for the child.

2.41 We also want to ensure that all local authorities have transparent policies in relation to the support they offer to family and friends carers, both via the care system and via section 17 of the Children Act 1989. In order to ensure that this is the case, we will:

- **Ask Ofsted to assess these policies as part of the Ofsted three year programme referred to in Chapter 1; and**

- **Provide guidance and, if necessary, amend the legislation to establish this framework.**

Residence orders

2.42 A residence order is an order available under the Children Act 1989 which is designed to settle the arrangements as to the person with whom a child will live. It confers parental responsibility on the holder of the residence order but does not extinguish the parental responsibility of those who already hold it, usually the birth parents.

2.43 Currently, while local authority foster carers who have had the child living with them for a year immediately preceding any application for a residence order are entitled to apply for one of these orders (without first obtaining the permission of the court), relative carers are not in the same position unless they are also already caring for the child or are a local authority foster carer; have had the child living with them for 3 out of the last 5 years, or have the consent of everyone with parental responsibility for the child. We believe that relative carers should also be able to apply after one year, even if they are not local authority foster carers and that the current provisions may act as an unnecessary obstacle. We will therefore:

- **Legislate to entitle relative carers to apply for a residence order if the child has lived with them for a continuous period of at least one year immediately preceding the application.**

2.44 It may be appropriate to bring the timescales for *applying* for special guardianship and adoption orders into line with this. We intend to explore further the implications of such changes with key stakeholders.

2.45 We will also ensure that any carers who are not the child's parents or guardians but who do have a residence order will retain parental responsibility for them until the child is 18. This will address the current problems faced by those carers who receive residence order allowances which cease on a child's sixteenth birthday. They then face a period of up to two years in which they are responsible for maintaining the child with no allowance while they complete their education.

2.46 This change is long overdue and is even more necessary if we are to realise the ambition of raising the age of participation in education and training. It is also important to bring it into line with other orders designed to secure children's futures such as Special Guardianship, an order available under the Adoption and Children Act 2002.

2.47 It is clear that Residence Orders and Special Guardianship Orders fulfil different purposes and we wish to limit any financial incentive to choose one route over the other to enable the best decision to be made in each individual case. We will:

- **Legislate to raise the age at which a residence order automatically ends from 16 to 18.**

Supporting the return home

2.48 Recent research evidence (Farmer et al)[7] has highlighted the lack of attention to supporting the return home of vulnerable children from care. In this study 46% of the children were re-abused or neglected after returning home. Key factors appeared to include a failure to work with birth families during the child's period in care and a failure to assess properly the safety of the parental and home circumstances prior to return. Many of the adults in these families have complex needs of their own as highlighted earlier in this chapter but it is essential that local authorities and partner agencies develop the skills and interventions to ensure that the welfare of children who have been in care is safeguarded upon their return home. In order to address these concerns we will:

- **Use the revised Children Act 1989 guidance to address the need for effective care planning to ensure that work continues with birth parents while the child is in care, and that appropriate services are delivered for the child and family to support return home, and**

- **Require all children who return home from care to have a Child in Need Plan which identifies areas in which parental capacity needs to be strengthened in order to safeguard the child on return home.** The plan will be reviewed regularly until the child is no longer considered a child in need. However, it may still be important to ensure

---

7   Elaine Farmer, Wendy Sturgess and Teresa O'Neill (forthcoming) 'The Reunification of Looked After Children with their Parents: Patterns, Interventions and Outcomes', Report to DfES, University of Bristol

that they are in receipt of other universal services such as those available through SureStart, Children's Centres and extended schools.

Wider context

2.49 The proposals described in this chapter are a part of a wider prevention agenda designed to ensure that families receive timely support and services to prevent problems becoming severe or entrenched and to reduce the short and long term impacts on children's development and well-being. A number of wider innovations are also in place or planned to support the delivery of these proposals for vulnerable children in general.

2.50 The implementation of the Common Assessment Framework (CAF) is providing an opportunity to identify vulnerable children and families and coordinate support at an earlier stage. It is also designed to reduce the need for unnecessary multiple assessments of families which can result in disengagement.

2.51 The implementation of the Integrated Children's System (ICS) for children identified as in need of services under the Children Act 1989 is improving assessment and care planning and providing a focus on appropriate and effective interventions for both child and family. The electronic system supports single data entry, reducing the burden of repetition for social workers, and allows greater flexibility between the 'child in need' and 'looked after' parts of the system, for example for children using short term breaks.

2.52 The care plan and review records require a specific focus on the outcomes of interventions in order to improve understanding of effectiveness. We want to support a smooth continuum of assessments and appropriate services in relation to the range of families' needs and will be looking at the relationship between the CAF and the ICS as implementation continues.

2.53 The development of ContactPoint[8] will enable multiple concerns to be identified by practitioners and ensure that children in highly mobile families who often have the greatest needs are not lost from view. ContactPoint provides an online directory which will provide a fast way for a practitioner to find out who else is working with the same child or young person.

2.54 A Centre for Excellence in Children's Services is also being developed, which will systematically gather, evaluate and share information on successful and innovative approaches across the breadth of children's services. While still in the early stages, our intention is to:

● **Develop further proposals for the Centre in consultation with key external stakeholders with a view to the centre beginning work early in 2008.**

8   www.everychildmatters.gov.uk/deliveringservices/contactpoint

Chapter 3
Care placements: a better experience for everyone

"I think a foster carer's personality is what makes a good foster carer. I am interested only in their kindness, understanding and commitment to me."

Young person

Summary

We need to ensure that children in care are provided with the one thing which they have told us makes the single biggest difference to their lives: being in the right placement. Building on the recommendations of the Placements Working Group, this chapter sets out a package of reforms for delivering a better choice of placements, and a more positive placement experience, by:

- Ensuring a strong focus on stability;

- Enabling local authorities to improve their commissioning of placements;

- Improving foster carer support and training;

- Better enforcing the National Minimum Standards for residential care;

- Piloting a 'social pedagogy' approach in residential care;

- Ensuring that children in long term residential placements in education or health settings get the best possible support;

- Improving practice in responding to children who go missing from care; and

- Ensuring that local authorities deliver a better placement experience for children in care, including a new set of regulations in relation to visits.

Introduction

3.1 We want all children in care to have kind, understanding and committed carers – whether foster carers or residential staff – and we want to encourage that element of 'stickability' which research has shown to be key to the successful continuation of relationships. The more engaged carers are in all aspects of the child's life and the greater their role in decision-making, the more likely they are to develop that close bond which will lead to a successful outcome for the child.

3.2 This means that the child and carer must be at the centre of all the activity and the work of the wider team around the child – the social worker, health professional, teacher – must be undertaken in a way which strengthens and supports the role of the carer rather than taking away responsibility.

3.3 Every placement decision must be based on a proper assessment of the child's needs and take account as far as possible of the child's wishes and feelings. Whether in foster care, residential care or placed with family/ friends carers, children and young people must be in placements which can meet the range of their individual needs – as far as possible close to home – and which support them on a personal level in leading a normal life and in developing the skills for a successful future.

3.4 This will not happen without a consistent focus on stability. Being subjected to successive moves of placement and school leads to a sense of rejection, loss of confidence and capacity to trust that ultimately reduce the child or young person's chances of settling with a family or in a children's home. Ensuring stability and continuity goes a long way to redressing the discontinuity and loss which many children have experienced before they enter care.

3.5 All placement decisions should be made with a view to maximising the opportunity for the child to find permanence. Where it is clear that a particular placement is temporary, the care plan should articulate what the longer term permanence option is and how the current placement will support its achievement.

Being available

Helping children to trust

The carer is available physically and emotionally to meet the child's needs whether they are together or apart.

This secure base helps the child to:
- feel safe
- trust that his or her needs will be met consistently
- gain the confidence to explore the world around them and learn
- learn to trust adults.

Responding sensitively	Helping children to manage feelings and behaviour
	The carer can 'stand in the child's shoes' and can think about what the child may be thinking and feeling, and can reflect this back to the child.
	They are also aware of their own feelings and can share these sensitively with the child.
	This helps the child to learn about and regulate his/her own feelings and to understand the thoughts and feelings of others.
Co-operative caring	Helping children to feel effective
	The carer is aware of the child as a separate person with wishes, feelings and goals and who needs to feel effective.
	The carer looks for ways to help the child feel more competent, such as by respecting the child's choices (within safe limits), using negotiation and co-operation to manage behaviour.
	This helps the child to feel his/her views are important and to learn to compromise and co-operate.
Accepting the child	Building self-esteem
	The carer gives the child the message that he or she is unconditionally accepted and valued for who they are, difficulties as well as strengths.
	The child learns that all people have some good and bad parts and that repair and forgiveness are possible.
	This helps the child to enjoy success and cope with setbacks.
Promoting family membership	Helping children to belong
	The carer has the capacity to include the child in their family for however long the child is to stay in their family.
	The carer also helps the child to belong to two families – his or her birth family and the family they are part of now, so that the child learns it is possible to belong to/love two families.

Taken from *Attachment Handbook for Foster Care and Adoption by Schofield and Beek, 2006*

3.6 Table 4.1 sets out the dimensions of parenting needed to help children become more confident and competent. Training and support services for carers should aim to develop and sustain these capacities which increase the likelihood of appropriate attachments developing.

A normal childhood

3.7 Children and young people told us very clearly through the consultation on the *Care Matters* Green Paper that while a focus on systems, placements and workforce is important, what is also crucial to them is that they are not singled out in front of their peers as being in care. We were told of numerous examples where children in placements were prevented from taking part in routine activities because of a series of rules and regulations – either perceived or real – which the carers and social workers were abiding by.

3.8 Children in care are necessarily subject to interventions in their lives which other children do not experience. However, we want to see such interventions delivered in as normal a way as possible to minimise the sense of difference which children in care often feel. For example, necessary health and safety requirements, particularly in children's homes, should not get in the way of children cooking and engaging in other activities which are essential for acquiring skills for life.

3.9 The Placement Information Record within the Integrated Children's System

(ICS) records the discussion which should happen at the start of any placement between the carer, child, social worker and, where appropriate, the birth parent about how the day to day parenting tasks will be carried out and what is appropriate to delegate to the carer. It is vital that this takes place, and that it takes into account the wishes and feelings of the child.

3.10 Children should, as far as possible, be granted the same permissions to take part in normal and acceptable age-appropriate activities as would reasonably be granted by the parents of their peers, and we would expect carers to behave as any other parent would in such situations. Local Authority Circular (2004) 4, which provides guidance on the delegation of decisions on overnight stays for children in care, is based on this principle. That guidance makes clear that the delegation of decisions about whether a particular child stays away from home is a matter which should be covered in the Foster Placement Agreement or the child's care or placement plan. The expectation is that children in care should be allowed to stay overnight with friends as other children would. However, agreements as to who is responsible for such decisions should be made on the basis of the vulnerability of the individual child.

3.11 Although there are risks in daily life for all children and young people, we cannot wrap children in cotton wool and prevent them from enjoying a normal childhood. This applies equally to children in care. The forthcoming consultation document *Staying Safe* will set out a strategy for Government to work with parents, children and young people and the wider community to raise awareness and understanding and enable everyone to play a role in keeping children safe from harm. The strategy will help to promote a better balance of risks and opportunities.

Commissioning

3.12 Good commissioning is crucial in raising the quality of placement provision, allowing good providers to flourish and providing an incentive for those who perform poorly to focus on improvement. If we are to succeed in our aim of improving children's experience of the care system then it is essential that effective strategies are in place at local and regional level.

3.13 We want to see local authorities use the information recorded about the needs of individual children within the ICS to provide aggregated information about their local population of children in need, including children in care. This will form the basis for developing the commissioning strategy for a range of provision to meet identified needs, from very local support foster care/short break care referred to in Chapter 2 to highly specialist residential care places or treatment foster care which may require regional commissioning. We will:

- **Impose a statutory duty on local authorities to secure a sufficient and diverse provision of quality placements within their local area.**

3.14 In considering the provision needed to satisfy this duty, local authorities will be required to consider the needs of particular groups of children such as disabled children and children from black and minority ethnic groups – including children of dual heritage. They will also need to consider gender differences in placement needs.

3.15 In order to ensure that the benefits of commissioning are delivered on a larger scale than a local authority area, we are:

- **Launching Regional Commissioning Unit Pilots.**

3.16 These pilots will support local authorities by ensuring that a menu of appropriate placements, tailored to meet the needs of the child, is available when the placement decision is being made. By contributing to greater placement choice, this approach will increase the likelihood of a placement being found which is well matched to the individual child. It will be especially helpful for children with complex needs, and disabled children. It will build, as far as possible, on existing support infrastructures within the region.

3.17 To strengthen further the ability of local authorities to commission sufficient appropriate placements, we will:

- **Issue guidance to help local authorities manage local placements markets, including**

publishing research on the optimal local supply of residential care.

3.18 We are also looking at ways to improve commissioning for very specialist placements such as those in secure children's homes. A significant number of secure children's homes have closed in recent years due, in part, to a drop in the number of children in care placed by local authorities in such settings.

3.19 We want to avoid a situation in which further home closures could lead to children being placed inappropriately in the community, where their needs will not be met. We will therefore:

- **Update guidance on the application of the Children Act 1989 for placements in secure children's homes.**

3.20 The criteria for placing a child in secure accommodation are already set out clearly in the Children Act 1989. Our guidance will make clear that, where these criteria are met, placement in a secure children's home should be a positive option for the children and young people concerned.

3.21 **We will also work with local authority partners and the Youth Justice Board to develop a wider strategy to explore the future demand for places for children in care in secure accommodation.** This will include looking at whether and how we might ensure a reasonable geographical distribution of secure children's homes so that children are not required to reside extremely long distances away

from their family home where this is not in their best interests. The Government will study the potential of the regional commissioning pilots or collaboration with other partners to play a role in managing such provision more effectively.

3.22 To enhance local authorities' commissioning capacity further, we will also:

- **Develop National Occupational Standards for service commissioners, working closely with Skills for Care and the Children's Workforce Development Council.**

3.23 In order to improve the way that local authorities contract with particular services, we are:

- **Supporting the development of a standardised national contract for residential care, in parallel with the existing national contract for independent and non-maintained special schools.** This will be available later in 2007 and will be voluntary. We are also looking at the possibility of developing a similar contract for Independent Fostering Agencies (IFAs).

Placement stability and support

3.24 A continued focus on stable placements is critical in order to achieve better outcomes. To this end, we commissioned the British Association for Adoption and Fostering (BAAF) to develop training materials for local authorities to audit their own performance, and to support them in taking action to improve the stability of particular groups of children they look after. The materials draw on recent work undertaken to address placement stability, and research by Professor Ian Sinclair of York University, which identified the various groups of children within the care population and how best to improve the stability of their placements. We will:

- **Ensure that these materials are made available to local authorities and to Government Offices later in 2007, to help support improvements to placement stability.**

3.25 The measures described above to support more effective commissioning of placements, better stability and greater placement choice will enable children to be better matched to placements and individual carers, thereby improving the likelihood of a placement succeeding. But a wide range of placements is not enough to make a placement succeed; ongoing training, development and support play a key role in reducing placement breakdown.

3.26 The *Care Matters* Green Paper set out our proposals for a tiered model of placement types for children in care, based on a three tier system. The model set out the skills which carers in each tier would need to care for children with particular levels of need: tier 1 corresponded to the least complex needs, and tier 3 the most complex. The

practical application of such a model was discussed in detail by the Placements Working Group, chaired by Lord Laming.

3.27 Members of the group did not consider that it was appropriate to base decisions about matching individual children to placements on this model. However, they agreed that the model had a useful role to play in informing the way in which placements were commissioned at a strategic level, and in providing a framework for the ongoing support, development and training of carers. In light of this, we will use this approach to inform our reforms to commissioning and carer training and support.

Foster care

3.28 In order for carers to provide the supportive commitment which is essential for children's development, they themselves must be provided with effective training and support. Carer stress, and the need to respond to difficult behaviour, account for a high proportion of placement breakdowns and instability for children.

3.29 The Children's Workforce Development Council has launched a set of Foster Care Training, Support and Development Standards which describe the skills and competences that all foster carers should be able to demonstrate. The Standards will play a key role in ensuring that providers make available to their carers appropriate opportunities for development, and that they support them in developing the skills and competences covered by the framework.

3.30 We intend to build on these standards and to develop them further, so that they take account of the competences needed to care for children with the most complex needs, and of other specialist developmental needs such as working with disabled young people or caring for teenage parents. We will also:

- **Use our planned revision of the National Minimum Standards for fostering services to establish a link with the new training and development standards.**

3.31 This will ensure that Ofsted, in its assessment of fostering services, considers how effectively providers are supporting their carers in reaching the agreed standards. This approach will allow us to put in place an agreed quality framework to underpin the approvals system for foster carers.

3.32 This framework for assessing the competences of carers will help to ensure that discussions between commissioners, providers and carers are more transparent. It will set out clearly the roles which carers are expected to fulfil and the skills which they need to develop. At the same time, it will provide the framework for the support and training which carers themselves may expect and it will give greater consistency to the way in which carers are assessed.

3.33 However, we intend to do more to equip carers to respond appropriately and positively to the children they care for. We will:

- **Fund a national rollout of the *Fostering Changes* Programme** by ensuring that those responsible for training foster carers are familiar with the programme and able to deliver the training to carers.

3.34 This programme, which was set up in 1999 by the Adoption and Fostering

North Somerset and Foster Carer Training

The North Somerset Training Department work with experienced foster carers to develop their skills as carers and as deliverers of training. When the authority began to train carers on the healthy care of children they involved a small team of carers to deliver the course in partnerships with the local health promotion unit and looked after children's nurse. This work has been in place for several years and is included as two modules of the "Skills to Foster" preparation course for foster carers. Carers have been supported by the training department to develop the training work and involve care experienced young people in delivering "Skills to Foster – health and wellbeing and Total Respect Training" for elected members and staff.

Carers involved in delivering the training have completed NVQ level 3, two have been supported to complete the FE certificate in adult learning and four are completing an online BTEC level 4 on "Caring for children with developmental trauma".

Specialist team at the South London and Maudsley Trust, provides practical advice using skills-based training for foster carers in order to develop their capacity to use positive parenting techniques to manage difficult and challenging child behaviour. A number of organisations are providing funding to BAAF to develop an additional module to this training to enable carers to support children's literacy skills.

3.35 We will also provide foster carers with guidance on providing high quality sex and relationships education to the young people in their care. This will focus on helping children and young people develop the confidence to resist pressure to have early sex and the knowledge and skills to prevent pregnancy. It will also help them look after their sexual health when they do become sexually active. The Healthy Care training manual contains good materials to support this work and the CWDC's Foster Care Training, Support and Development Standards already include sexual health promotion.

Enabling consistency of care across the country

3.36 The role of foster carers is extremely challenging; the diverse needs of the children in foster care require a range of skills and it is essential that training and support are available to ensure that carers are properly equipped with these skills. We also intend to:

- **Establish robust systems to ensure that foster carers' skills, training and qualifications are properly recorded, and that this information is available to new fostering service providers if the carer moves.**

3.37 In doing so, we are seeking to reinforce the importance placed on the development of foster carers' skills; to establish greater consistency in the way in which skills are assessed and recorded; and to make available to all fostering service providers details of individual carers' skills and training, so that when foster carers move between agencies details of their previous achievements are not lost. We will also:

- **Provide for the exchange of information between agencies**, by requiring a new provider to seek information from a previous provider about a prospective carer, and by requiring the previous provider to comply with such a request.

3.38 We know that the lack of an independent appeals mechanism is also a concern for those applying to be foster carers. We therefore intend to:

- **Extend the existing Independent Review Mechanism – which considers applications from prospective adopters for reviews of an adoption agency determination that they are not suitable to adopt or to withdraw their earlier approval – to prospective foster carers.**

Multi-dimensional Treatment Foster Care

3.39 The pilot programme of Multi-dimensional Treatment Foster Care for adolescents with complex needs and challenging behaviour is beginning to show promising improvements in outcomes for young people who have been in the programme. These programmes are being developed alongside the Youth Justice Board Intensive Fostering programme, which uses the same model.

3.40 We are, therefore, now at the stage where we are able to consider how aspects of this specialist model could benefit wider groups of foster carers. The value of such an approach is highlighted by recent research from the Oregon Social Learning Centre's KEEP project, which identified a systematic way of anticipating likely placement disruptions. It showed that when carers reported more than 5 daily incidences of behaviour which the carer found stressful, it was a strong predictor that a placement may break down. We will therefore:

- **Fund pilot sites to test the use of a weekly foster carer meeting and a Weekly Parent Report on behaviour in order to anticipate the likelihood of placement disruption and to provide appropriate intervention and support.**

3.41 We are supporting the development of Multi-dimensional Treatment Foster Care pilots for young children, using the lessons from pilots for adolescents to make more effective use of parenting interventions to support the successful return home of children from care or to support effective permanence arrangements in a new family . We have awarded pump-priming funding to six local authorities and their partners and the first placements will be made later in 2007.

Payments for foster carers

3.42 It would not be appropriate to set out at a national level exactly which training courses each residential or foster care service should offer its carers, nor the level of funding which each carer should receive, precisely because we know there are significant variations of need across the country and the role of carers is so diverse. However, foster carers have told us that they often do not know what the local authority's policy on payments is, and the Placements Working Group highlighted the importance of every local authority having in place an effective policy on payments to carers. We will therefore:

- **Require all fostering services to publish details of their payment structures for foster carers, in relation to the nature of the task being undertaken and the level of training required.**

3.43 Such an approach will offer a clearer and more consistent approach to understanding foster carers' needs and provide a framework for raising the quality of the workforce.

Tesco staff training to become foster carers

Tesco and the union Usdaw have struck a pioneering agreement that will give Tesco employees a one-off allowance of up to five days paid leave for those who want to become foster parents. The policy was launched in April 2007. These five days can be used by staff to undertake the detailed application process, attend foster care related meetings or complete specialised training.

The idea of paid leave for foster carers was raised by Usdaw members in one store, and Tesco agreed to this new policy after staff raised the issue through the consultative forum of the Usdaw/Tesco Partnership Agreement.

The agreement has significant benefits both for children in care, who need dedicated, well-trained foster carers, and for Tesco staff who wish to become foster carers.

Tesco believes that this initiative will contribute to the retention of loyal staff by supporting employees who want to take on this vital role. The initiative is part of an ongoing commitment by Usdaw and Tesco to work together to deliver family friendly policies for the Tesco workforce.

Foster carer recruitment

3.44 We know that recruitment of foster carers is most effective when done locally and we expect local authorities to be engaging with their local communities to highlight the different ways in which individuals can become involved in supporting vulnerable children. But local authorities and other stakeholders tell us that more could be done to increase awareness and understanding of the issues involved in caring for children in care. We will therefore:

- **Support a campaign to raise the profile of foster care nationally, and to support local initiatives in recruiting more foster carers.**

Permanence

3.45 The overarching purpose of care is to support children to find permanence.

This White Paper sets out ways to improve the options for children, whether to return home, to live with wider family and friends or with a long term foster carer or a special guardian, to remain in residential care or to be adopted. There should be no disincentives attached to any one option or another.

3.46 Consultation with children and young people has highlighted a number of issues relevant to permanence planning, including the importance of not separating siblings without a full assessment both of their views and of the implications of the separation. This must be taken into account where a permanent placement is being considered which would result in a child being separated from his or her siblings. Children did not necessarily view adoption as their preferred option, but felt that all options should be considered. Young people also indicated that in many cases they would prefer to be in a long-term foster placement, in order to preserve ties with their birth families.

Special Guardianship

3.47 The Adoption and Children 2002 Act introduced **special guardianship** orders to provide permanence for children who cannot return to their birth families, but for whom adoption is not the most suitable option. Special guardianship is a legally secure permanence option for children, without the absolute legal severance from the birth family that stems from an adoption order. It is expected that foster carers and children in long term foster placements, minority ethnic communities with religious and cultural difficulties with adoption, carers who are relatives and older children who do not want to sever legal ties with their birth family, will benefit particularly from special guardianship.

3.48 A special guardian is able to exercise parental responsibility to the exclusion of all others (but cannot consent to adoption). This puts the day to day upbringing of the child firmly in the hands of the special guardian. Special guardianship is accompanied by a full range of support services which mirror those available for adoption, including, where appropriate, financial support, to ensure the success of this permanence option.

Adoption

3.49 **Adoption** provides an important opportunity for some children who cannot live with their birth family to be part of a permanent and loving family. The Adoption and Children Act 2002 came fully into force on 30 December 2005, modernising the whole legal framework for adoption and encouraging and enabling more people to adopt. Single people, unmarried couples (irrespective of their sexuality), civil partners and married couples are now able to apply to adopt a child, widening the pool of potential adoptive parents and thereby ensuring that more vulnerable children will have the chance of the family life that adoption can bring.

3.50 The 2002 Act aims also to encourage and enable more people to adopt children from care by helping ensure that the range of support services they might need are available. The Adoption Register in England and Wales enables children and prospective adopters to be matched beyond local areas. It has an important role to play in finding matches for more difficult to place children, such as those in sibling groups.

3.51 The Future of the Care Population Working Group Report recommended that Government require all local authorities to review their use of adoption and special guardianship. Adoption agencies (local authorities and voluntary adoption agencies) are already required to keep under review the adoption service they provide.

Planned further training to support implementation of the 2002 Act, that will have a particular focus on special guardianship, will encourage local authorities to reflect on the range of permanence options available in planning for individual children.

Concurrent planning

3.52 Concurrent planning can provide a way in which young children can achieve permanence with the minimum of placement moves. In concurrent planning arrangements, a child in care is placed with approved foster carers who, as well as providing temporary care for the child, bring him/her to regular supervised contact sessions with his/her birth parents and other relatives. The carers are also approved as prospective adopters so that if the birth parents' rehabilitation plan is not successful, the child does not need to move when the care plan changes and

Ruth's story

Ruth was born drug-addicted. She spent the first three months of her life on a busy hospital ward undergoing a drug-detoxification programme. Ruth's parents, Linda and Joe, were initially keen to overcome their difficulties in order to care for Ruth. However, within days of Ruth's birth they ceased visiting her in hospital. Ruth started life in great physical discomfort and without any special adults around with whom she could form a loving bond and attachment.

Both Linda and Joe's own childhoods had been abusive. At the time of Ruth's birth, Linda and Joe had both been using street drugs for many years. Linda's five previous children had all been removed from her care. Joe and Linda were advised that the Concurrent Planning Project would support them as much as possible to overcome their drug-related difficulties, but that they would need to begin to address these immediately. The couple accepted that Ruth should be placed with Concurrent carers in the meantime.

Joe and Linda agreed to work with the Project. However, they soon began to miss appointments and began to avoid contact with all professionals. Joe was evicted from their hostel as a result of his aggressive behaviour. When Ruth was four months old Linda fell from a 6th floor window and was admitted to hospital for several weeks. At this point Joe disappeared.

Concurrent Planning carers Caron and Rod began daily hospital visits to Ruth, so she could get to know them and to build up trust. Ruth was discharged from hospital to their care aged 3 months. Initially Linda was reluctant to meet Caron and Rod, but having done so formed a good relationship with them. Linda was pleased that Ruth was receiving good care and accepted that she could not care for Ruth herself. Caron and Rod adopted Ruth when she was 12 months old, having been in her life since she was 3 weeks old. Within a week of her discharge from hospital Linda disappeared and has not been in contact since then. Rod and Caron remain open to future contact with her, and with Joe, for Ruth's sake.

can remain in the same placement while his/her adoption plan is developed and implemented.

3.54 Concurrent planning has the potential to benefit those children in care for whom reunification with their birth parents does not look promising but where it cannot yet be ruled out and who will need an adoptive family if reunification is not successful. Its purpose is to prevent children from drifting in care and becoming harder to place because they have suffered placement breakdown and disrupted attachments.

3.55 Concurrent planning is not the right option for all children and we should not overestimate its potential. It needs to be seen in the wider context of care planning, as one of a number of options for achieving permanence. However, it can offer significant benefits for a small group of children.

3.55 There are currently four concurrent planning projects in England: two of which are provided by voluntary adoption agencies – the Coram Family (in London) and the Manchester Adoption Society; and two of which are provided by local authorities – Brighton & Hove, and Kent. Devon Council is about to start a pilot project.

3.56 The Government is committed to promoting and enabling greater use of concurrent planning, including by raising awareness of its benefits and limitations, the availability of existing services and the learning from these projects. We will do this in part through:

- **Ensuring that social worker training includes a component on effective concurrent planning; and**

- **Issuing guidance for those social workers with responsibility for permanence planning.**

Residential care

3.57 Our expectation is that most children will benefit from being in a family setting, as has been the thrust of Government policy in recent years. As a result, more children than ever before are in foster care placements. Nevertheless, residential care has an important role to play as part of a range of placement options. For a significant number of children – particularly older children – a residential placement will be the right choice. In other cases too, residential care has a role to play in enabling other placement types to succeed – it may, for example, be used to provide a valuable bridge for young people who are not ready to settle in a family placement. It will not necessarily be the case that a child must be placed solely in a foster placement or solely in residential care – it may be that a combination of the two is the right choice for some.

3.58 It is therefore essential that our reforms focus on ensuring that the residential sector provides good quality care and that it is a valued and dynamic setting, able to support children in their development and enable them to move on where that is appropriate. Residential care workers must therefore be

Education in a children's home

St. Christopher's residential unit has put education at the heart of its approach – working in partnership with Connexions, education teams and community organisations to provide education support packages tailored to the needs of its residents.

An education co-ordinator has been appointed to manage the education provision and a dedicated 'tuition room' set aside for learning activities. One resident, Steve, is a 16 year old boy with a statement of special educational needs and significant behavioural difficulties. It has been difficult to find a school place that meets his needs and there have been problems with bullying and poor attendance.

St. Christopher's arranged one to one tuition and support from a Learning Support Assistant for Steve – support is co-ordinated by Steve's keyworker who liaises with other professionals on his behalf. Connexions have identified vocational courses in sports and painting and decorating which match Steve's interests and he is currently performing well. His ability to undertake structured programmes of this sort is a positive indicator for his future.

St. Christopher's plan to continue the focus on supporting resident's education, ensuring it is fully incorporated into care planning and increasing integration with mainstream education.

appropriately trained and able to support young people on a range of issues, such as education and health, including those relating to sexual health and relationships advice. We will consider with Children's Workforce Development Council how we can best support residential workers in fulfilling this role and will look further at pathways available to residential care staff.

Social pedagogy

3.59 Social pedagogy provides a theoretical and practical framework for understanding children's upbringing. It has a particular focus on building relationships through practical engagement with children and young people using skills such as art and music or outdoor activities. It provides the foundation for training those working with children in many other European countries. In a residential care setting, it brings a particular expertise in working with groups and using the group as a support. In order to explore ways to improve the quality of care on offer, we will:

● **Fund a pilot programme to evaluate the effectiveness of social pedagogy in residential care.**

3.60 In recent years, a number of children's residential homes in England have employed Danish and German pedagogues and reported very positive experiences for children and young people and staff members. The pilots we are proposing will build on this experience to provide answers to key questions about the impact of implementing a model in a new cultural and practice context. They will also assess the impact on outcomes for children and the experience of the children and young people.

Improving the quality of residential care

3.61 Currently only a quarter of homes meet 90% or more of the National Minimum Standards. This level of performance is unacceptable and we will take strong measures to address the issue of under-performance in children's homes. Whilst the proportion of local authority run homes meeting National Minimum Standards is lower than those run by the voluntary or private sector, the level of performance across all sectors raises serious concerns. We will:

- **Give Ofsted an express power, in cases where a provider is failing to comply with the relevant regulatory requirements, to issue a notice setting out the details of the failure, the action needed to address it and the timescale within which action must be taken.**

3.62 This approach will focus attention on the action needed to address any shortcomings. Young people themselves have expressed their desire to see poor performing children's homes given the opportunity to improve before any consideration of

closure, since closure of the home is likely to have a significant cost to the children placed there. Failure to comply with the terms of a notice may, however, lead to further action in the form of prosecution or de-registration.

3.63 And, under the approach we are proposing, all Directors of Children's Services will be informed by Ofsted of non-compliance with a notice served by Ofsted, and of certain other enforcement action which is being taken against a provider. Those authorities which have already placed children will be required to conduct a risk assessment and consider, taking account of the wishes of the child concerned, whether that placement remains appropriate. Other local authorities will be able to take account of this information in considering any new placements.

3.64 Our commitment to raising standards applies to all settings where children are placed and it is therefore our intention to mirror the approach described above in other children's settings registered under the Care Standards Act 2000, including independent fostering providers and residential family centres.

3.65 In some cases, concerns about performance will be such that we would wish to ensure that no new placements could be made. In order to achieve this we will also **give Ofsted the statutory power to prevent further admissions from taking place**.

Out of authority placements

3.66 As previously discussed, we are looking to encourage a diversity of provision within local authority areas, which is sufficient to meet the needs of all children in care. The recent change in establishing the responsible Primary Care Trust (PCT) commissioner regulations for children in care should help to encourage local placements.

3.67 Children and young people have told us that they can feel isolated in distant placements and miss contact with their friends and with their local communities. They also feel that they may not be able to depend on regular visits from their social workers to make sure that plans for their future care reflect their wishes and feelings. We know too from the work of the Children's Rights Director that some children placed out of their local authority have been threatened with the abrupt ending of their out of authority placements even though they feel settled and happy.

3.68 However, assessment of some children's needs may still result in a placement away from their local authority area, where the local authority can demonstrate that the child's needs will best met by a specialist out-of-area placement. We have already highlighted the importance of regional or sub-regional commissioning for children with very specialist needs, including treatment needs.

3.69 We know that children placed out of their local authority may be particularly vulnerable to poor outcomes. These children often have difficulty being able to access appropriate local services so that, for example, they may not get the right support to help them with their education, or may not be able to use local Child and Adolescent Mental Health Services. Effective commissioning is needed to ensure that these issues are addressed.

3.70 Where an out of authority placement is being considered, it will be important that this option is discussed with the child and, wherever possible, that he or she is supported in visiting before being expected to move in to the new placement. In these circumstances, the placing local authority is responsible for forming the necessary relationships with the child's school and with other local services and the child's social worker should visit the child regularly and often. Whenever a placement has to be made out of authority then the child must be provided with the same level of support that he or she could have expected had it been possible to find a placement closer to home.

3.71 We will:

- **Strengthen the statutory framework so that a local authority may not place a child out of its local authority area unless it is satisfied that such a placement is in the child's best interests.**

3.72 Alongside this, revisions to the regulatory framework governing care planning for children in care will:

- **Set out a rigorous process that must be followed so that any decision to place a child out of their authority is scrutinised and agreed at a senior level of the local authority's children's services;**

- **Specify the mutual responsibilities of placing authorities and area authorities;**

- **Confirm that where any child is placed out of authority, he/she should only be removed from that placement and placed closer to home if the move is assessed as better able to meet the full range of the child's needs, and the child's own views have been sought and taken into account; and**

- **Describe the arrangements to be followed in relation to emergency placements.**

Disabled children in long term residential placements

3.73 Children in long term residential placements in health or education settings are known to be vulnerable, especially where the placement is a 52 week placement. The circumstances around the placement – including the involvement of the child's parents – may well change over time. However, the impact of such changes is not always adequately assessed and addressed. Consultation responses to the *Care Matters* Green Paper indicate clearly the importance of supporting

the role of parents, and not undermining it. At the same time, it is essential that appropriate measures to safeguard and promote the welfare of children are in place.

3.74 We will therefore improve and strengthen the way in which local authorities supervise these placements. We will achieve this in part by:

- **Clarifying the current requirement for placing agencies to notify the local authority concerned of the placement**, in order to ensure that the notification is addressed to the DCS;

- **Introducing a requirement for the local authority in which the child is ordinarily resident to visit and maintain contact with children in such placements**, to help ensure that a child's ongoing needs are met, not just at the point of placement but in the event of any change of circumstances during the placement; and

- **Issuing guidance setting out the role and purpose of the visit.**

3.75 The guidance will underline our existing expectation that children who are in longterm residential placements which are funded primarily by local authorities should, in the vast majority of cases, be looked after. Only in those cases where, having undertaken an assessment of need, the authority is satisfied that there is a high ongoing level of parental engagement and support for the child should looked after status not apply. This package will ensure that local authorities consider, in consultation with parents, whether it is appropriate in the circumstances for the child to be legally looked after by the local authority.

Children missing from care

3.76 The Government published *Children Missing from Care and Home – a guide to good practice* in tandem with the Social Exclusion Unit's report *Young Runaways* in November 2002. This was issued as statutory guidance which must be followed by local authorities except in exceptional circumstances.

3.77 This guidance requires local authorities to appoint a senior manager to monitor 'missing from care' incidents, so that trends in children being absent from care can be identified and any necessary action can be taken to minimise patterns of young people going missing. Furthermore, the National Minimum Standards for Children's Homes and Fostering Services require that all homes and fostering services should have explicit procedures to follow when children in their care may be missing or absent. However, we recognise that, unfortunately, a minority of children continue to feel the need to run away and go missing from their care placements.

3.78 Improvements we are putting in place, including the greater focus on meeting children's needs and the drive to raise standards, will reduce the likelihood of young people running away from care.

But, building on previous guidance, we will be taking further steps to tackle this issue. In particular, we will:

● **Use the forthcoming beacons scheme for children in care to ensure the effective sharing of good practice;**

● **Ensure through the effective implementation of the Integrated Children's System roll out that effective contingency arrangements are prompted** in relation to the care plans for children who have a history of running away;

● **Ensure that the revised NMS put the right emphasis on the need to reduce the risk of children going missing** and the necessity for all children's homes to follow local police procedures for reporting missing persons and managing missing from care incidents;

● **Ensure that the revised Children Act Guidance covers this issue:**

  – to emphasise the importance of assessing the risk of harm to self or others of young people going missing, and put in place proper preventive strategies;

  – to highlight the role of corporate parents in taking prompt and decisive action should children in care go missing;

  – to emphasise the need for each child returning to have the opportunity to be debriefed on any reasons for their running away – to a person independent of their placement and in their own time – with any indicated action taken in the child's interests; and

- to reinforce the importance of systematic recording and data collection.

- Explore with Ofsted how **this will be reflected in inspection arrangements**;

- **Ensure that the proposed Annual National Stocktake reflects this issue.** This could be used to identify trends and to identify local authorities with a particular problem in this area; and

- Work with the Home Office to ensure that the specific needs of unaccompanied asylum seeking children who go missing from care are reflected.

Visits

3.79 All children and young people in care, regardless of the type of placement they are in, must be in settings which meet their needs, and which support them in leading a normal life and in developing their skills for a successful future. Regular contact between the child and a social worker is extremely important in ensuring that a placement continues to meet the child's needs. Of course, the circumstances, feelings and difficulties which a child may wish to discuss with his or her social worker do not necessarily coincide with regular prescribed visits. For that reason, it is essential that children in care are able to contact their social worker between visits.

3.80 The requirements of the current regulatory framework, particularly in relation to the consideration which must be given to children's views, already imply that children in all types of placements are visited, and that local authorities should provide ways for children in care to contact their social workers in between these visits. In some cases, such as fostering, the regulations already set out explicit requirements relating to visits. Worryingly, however, young people have told us that visits do not always take place, and have reiterated how important these visits are to them. This can be particularly acute when young people in care go into custody.

3.81 We will therefore:

- **Make the requirement to visit children in care explicit for all placements; and**

- **Introduce a requirement that social workers visiting children in placements will normally see the child alone and away from their carers.**

3.82 We recognise that the frequency of visits will depend on the individual child's needs and that some children will require more frequent visits than others. Children's social workers are best placed to make this assessment. In addition, we will:

- **Introduce an explicit requirement for local authorities to ensure that**

young people have appropriate opportunities to contact their social worker and seek advice outside these visits; and

- **Extend the requirement to visit children in care to those children who were voluntarily accommodated immediately before entering custody.** This provides a mechanism to identify those young people who should have a needs assessment so that where necessary local authority children's services makes proper plans for them on release; which could include working with the YOT to support the young person and their family in the community, or readmitting the young person to care.

3.83 This will ensure that this small group of vulnerable young people have access to advice and support and, importantly, that the responsible local authority is planning for their release – including where appropriate planning for provision of accommodation and other services. We will also:

- **Introduce a notification requirement so that Youth Offending Teams must inform the responsible local authorities where their children in care, whether or not they share formal parental responsibility for them, enter custody**, so that the authority ensures that they are visited and children are not forgotten about whilst in custody.

Chapter 4
Delivering a first class education

"I have personal experience of having a designated teacher. It can work."

Young person

Summary

Getting a first class education is vital to improving outcomes for children in care. It acts as the foundation for improving outcomes throughout their lives. To improve the education of children in care we are:

- **Improving access to high quality early years provision;**

- **Ensuring children in care have access to the best schools through priority in admissions arrangements and a presumption that they will not move schools;**

- **Personalising their learning through: better assessment and intervention; a personal learning allowance of £500; personal tutoring; improved 14-19 provision; and extended activities;**

- **Putting the designated teacher on a statutory footing and introducing virtual school heads to improve provision in schools;**

- **Taking targeted action on poor attendance and strengthening guidance on exclusion of children in care – making it clear that it should be an absolute last resort;**

- **Improving support for carers, including training for foster carers; and**

- **Improving accountability.**

Introduction

4.1   A high quality education provides the foundation for transforming the lives of children in care. Children and young people in care have told us how important education is to their lives.

Children who leave care with no qualifications are less likely to be in education, employment or training, are five times more likely than those with qualifications to be in custody at age 19 and are nearly twice as likely to have lost touch with the local authority that supported them.

4.2 Since 1997 the Government has made a good education for every children and young person a top priority, and standards have risen significantly. Primary standards are at their highest ever levels and record numbers of 16 year olds are achieving five good grades at GCSE (A*-C or equivalent). Investment in schools has risen by £25 billion since 1997.

4.3 We have made great strides in a comprehensive reform of the school workforce, increasing the number of full-time equivalent (FTE) teachers by over 35,500 and more than doubling the number of FTE support staff to 305,500. We are reforming the National Curriculum and introducing diplomas at 14-19, so that children and young people are better engaged with and motivated by their learning. The Children Act 2004 placed local authorities under a duty to promote the educational achievement of children in care.

4.4 Children in care face a number of barriers to their education. It is often interrupted – and we know that stability of care and educational placements is key to raising attainment. They may not receive adequate support for their learning at home and they experience significantly higher rates of special educational needs than other children. However, even accounting for these

barriers, educational outcomes have not improved sufficiently. In 2006, only 12% of children in care achieved 5A*-C at GCSE, or equivalent – significantly lower than their peers and shocking for 21st century Britain.

4.5 The *Care Matters* Green Paper set out a range of proposals to give children in care a first class education that allows them to reach their potential. We established the Best Practice in Schools Working Group, chaired by Dame Pat Collarbone, to explore ways of improving the education of children in care. Consultation on the *Care Matters* Green Paper demonstrated strong support for the proposals it contained.

Early years

4.6 Evidence shows the difference that high quality early years provision makes in improving outcomes for children, particularly disadvantaged children[1] and it is vital that children in care share the opportunities afforded by high quality early years provision.

4.7 We have invested over £21 billion in transforming early learning and childcare, more than doubling the stock of registered childcare places and introducing a free entitlement to early years education for all three and four year olds. The Childcare Act 2006 introduced a duty on local authorities, working with their NHS and Jobcentre Plus partners, to improve the outcomes of all young children aged 0-5 and

---

1 P Sammons et al (2007) Effective Pre-school and Primary Education 3-11 Project (EPPE 3-11), *Summary Report Influences on Children's Attainment and Progress in Key Stage 2: Cognitive Outcomes in Year 5.* DfES Research Report RR828.

reduce inequalities between them. Sure Start Children's Centres are providing early education and care; health and family support services; access to employment opportunities and training for parents and carers. We now have over 1,300 children's centres, on course for 3,500 by 2010 – one for every community.

4.8 However, at present, children in care are less likely than their peers to benefit from high quality early years provision. It is vital that those caring for children understand the importance of this stage of development.

4.9 From April 2008 local authorities will be under a duty to provide information, advice and assistance to parents and carers in finding appropriate early years provision. We will set out in statutory guidance how, in fulfilling this duty, local authorities should ensure that key people working with children in care have access to the same information as is available to parents. New standards for foster carers (see Chapter 3) outline the importance of understanding the benefits of early years provision and will be linked to revised National Minimum Standards, to be published in 2009.

4.10 Local authorities are well placed to ensure that all young children in care benefit from good quality early years education and care. Decisions on appropriate provision for children in care must always be based on the individual needs of the child. However, research has shown that for most children high quality early education is vital to their development. We will therefore:

- **Introduce an expectation in care planning arrangements for children under five, particularly those aged three and four, that, except where it is demonstrated that it is not in the child's best interests, the social worker will work with the carer and the local authority to arrange high-quality early years education as part of the child's care plan.**

Admissions

4.11 *Care Matters* showed how children in care are disproportionately less likely than their peers to be in high-performing schools with a consequent impact on their education. Across the education system total recurrent funding per pupil has increased by 66% in real terms since 1997 to help make every school a good school. Schools are able to offer a better, more personalised, education, and curriculum and qualifications reform is helping to ensure that all children and young people engage with learning. Local authorities also have new powers, as the guarantor of high standards, to intervene where provision is poor.

4.12 Local authorities, as corporate parents, should use their powers to ensure that children and young people in care have access to high quality education, which best meets their needs. The law requires that children in care must be given top priority in published admission arrangements for maintained schools and Academies. Building on this, **the Education and Inspections Act 2006 gave local authorities the power to direct schools to admit children in care, even where the school is already fully subscribed**.

4.13 Local admission forums must promote the needs of children in care and where they produce an annual report they must include information on the admission of children in care. Building on this:

- **The Schools' Commissioner will report in January 2009 on admission arrangements for children in care – including the use of local authority powers – as part of his report on fair admissions.**

Boarding Schools

4.14 Boarding schools can provide a stable, high quality education as well as the strong support for social and emotional development that is necessary to meet the needs of vulnerable children, including children in care. Boarding schools can also offer excellent support outside the classroom and a wide range of sporting and other activities which we know are crucial to positive outcomes. Some local authorities already use boarding or other residential schools for some of their children in care.

4.15 A majority of children and young people and professionals working with children in care feel that children in care should be given the opportunity to consider boarding school as an alternative placement[2]. However, concerns have also been raised that boarding school should not become a fall back position for placing children in care. Children and young people were also concerned that they should be able to maintain contact with their family and friends. Decisions must be taken in the best interests of the child or young person, but for some children in care boarding school could provide a good start in life.

4.16 The Department for Education and Skills is currently working with educational charitable trusts, 10 local authorities and 60 state maintained and independent boarding schools to test the effectiveness of boarding provision for vulnerable children. We will explore what further support local authorities and schools need in developing their provision. Building on the pilots we will work with local authorities to promote better access and availability for those children where the assessment of the child's needs indicates that boarding provision would be beneficial.

Stability of schooling

4.17 Stability is fundamental to ensuring a good education for all children. However, too many children in care experience multiple placements – just

---

2   *Care Matters: Consultation Responses*, Department for Education and Skills (2007)

over one in 10 children leaving care in the year ending 31 March 2006 had nine or more placements whilst in care and only 65% of children who had been in care for over two and a half years had been in the same placement for two years or more.

4.18 Consequently, and also as a result of exclusion, children in care also experience too many changes of school place. Evidence shows the impact that this mobility has on their education. On average, pupils who move schools during Key Stage 4 attain 75 points lower at GCSE – equivalent to between one and two grades in every subject – even after factors such as prior attainment and deprivation are taken into account[3].

4.19 We will, therefore, reduce the disruption of school for children in care by:

- **Legislating to introduce a requirement that the local authority must ensure that a child or young person's education is not disrupted as a result of care planning decisions. This will include a specific requirement that children in care must not move schools in years 10 and 11, except in exceptional circumstances.**

4.20 To support this, we will make clear to local authorities, through our revised Children Act 1989 Guidance, that the cost of transport, including for disabled children who may face particular transport barriers, should not act as a barrier to children in care remaining in a school placement. Where necessary, the local authority should provide free school transport.

4.21 Some school moves are the result of poor care planning decisions by the local authority, and social workers do not always take account of the impact of their decisions on education. It is vital that children's services work together support improvements to the education of children in care. Decisions about where children will live should include consideration of the importance of providing continuity of education. This stability is also vital to continuity of friendships and wider social relationships, which are key to developing children and young people's resilience.

4.22 As part of improving the training of social workers, outlined in Chapter 7, **we will ensure that they develop their understanding of the importance of education and social relationships.** Our revised guidance on care planning will **set out how the care planning process should emphasise the importance of education and ensure that care planning decisions do not adversely impact on educational stability**.

4.23 Chapter 3 sets out how we will restrict out of authority placements, unless there is evidence that such a placement is in the best interests of the child.

---

3   DfES contextualised Key Stage 2-4 value added model (2006): http://www.dfes.gov.uk/performancetables/schools_06/s12.shtml

However, for those children who are placed out of authority it is vital that the placing local authority considers the educational implications of such a placement.

4.24 Statutory guidance[4] already makes it clear that children placed out of authority should have an opportunity to visit both their care and new educational placement before they move and that social worker visits should be regular and planned. We will strengthen the procedures for making an out of authority placement so that children placed out of authority receive the same level of educational support as any other child in care.

Designated teacher

4.25 The quality of education can have a dramatic impact on outcomes for children and young people in care. Schools with clear accountability for raising the attainment of children in care, along with effective pastoral support and good links with other children's services, are in the best position to raise the attainment of children in care.

4.26 Many schools have appointed a 'designated teacher' for children in care. Having a teacher who understands the needs of children in care, takes responsibility for raising their attainment, analyses data and identifies their learning needs, and puts in place appropriate teaching and learning provision, can have a marked impact on their education. Designated teachers should ensure the progression of all children in care in the school; leading work with colleagues to make sure that provision is put in place to aid continual progress, as well as working with children's carers and promoting good home-school links.

4.27 Children and young people in care often have a number of professionals involved in their lives. Designated teachers provide the important link between the school, the child or young person's lead professional and social worker[5], the virtual school head (see page 71) and other children's services. The designated teacher should lead work to improve their attainment, in particular through input into their personal education plan. Local authorities should provide training for designated teachers, including multi-agency training with social workers – enabling professionals to work together better to support the education of children in care.

4.28 Children and young people have mixed views on the current effectiveness of designated teachers and some do not even know the role exists[6]. To ensure universal provision of designated teachers and improve their effectiveness, the Care Matters Green

---

4   Statutory guidance on the duty on local authorities to promote the educational achievement of looked after children under section 52 of the Children Act 2004, DfES (2005)

5   For children in care the lead professional role is usually carried out by their social worker.

6   Care Matters: Consultation Responses, Department for Education and Skills (2007)

Designated teacher

Jennifer is in year 10 and has been in care since she was 7 years old. Her two younger brothers have moved successfully into adoptive families. However, she remains traumatised by her pre-care experiences and has always struggled with relationships with adults and peers and, although bright, has found school challenging.

Jennifer's designated teacher is extremely pro-active. She attends all local authority and personal education plan reviews. Since year 7, she has met with Jennifer at least weekly, to discuss her progress at school. She has mediated frequently on Jennifer's behalf in difficulties in the school and has delivered training and advice to her colleagues on the needs of children in care in general and Jennifer in particular. She has encouraged all staff to 'go the extra mile' for Jennifer and has never shown frustration or despair when Jennifer's actions and reactions have caused difficulties for Jennifer herself and others.

After Key Stage 3, she worked with Jennifer to arrange courses for GCSE that Jennifer felt she would enjoy and be motivated to complete. She is now taking courses that will result in 9 GCSEs. Without this support Jennifer would have experienced exclusions and breaks in her learning, reducing her chances of success. As it is, she is managing to maintain a group of friends and a full timetable of learning.

Paper proposed to put the role of designated teacher on a statutory footing. This proposal was widely supported in consultation responses and by the Best Practice in Schools Working Group. We will therefore:

- **Legislate to put the role of designated teacher on a statutory footing, supported by training and statutory guidance clearly setting out their role and responsibilities. This will apply to new Academies through their funding agreements.**

4.29 The Best Practice in Schools Working Group concluded that to ensure they can represent children in care effectively, the designated teacher should be a member of the school's senior leadership team and will normally be a qualified teacher. We

recognise that, in line with the school workforce agreement, schools have been remodelling themselves in ways that mean not all aspects of the job need necessarily be carried out by a single individual or indeed by a qualified teacher.

4.30 Nevertheless, given the central importance we attach to the quality of teaching and learning experienced by every child in care and the relationship that has to the standards they achieve and the progress they make, **we will specify that the role should be carried out by a teacher**. Schools should determine where precisely in their structure this would best locate the role and how functions within it, including pastoral and more administrative tasks, are most appropriately delegated.

The personal education plan

4.31 A key aspect of the designated teacher's role is their involvement in the design and delivery of Personal Education Plans (PEP). All children in care should have a PEP covering a record of their achievements, identification of their educational and developmental needs, clear attainment targets, and long term plans and aspirations. It should set out what is needed to ensure the progression of each child or young person in care. Since 2005 the PEP has formed part of the official school record for children in care. It is important that social workers and the designated teacher work together to ensure that children, young people and their carers are involved in the planning of PEPs and that their views are heard and their interests represented.

4.32 A PEP is not a substitute for a good relationship between the designated teacher and the social worker. However, a high quality PEP can help teachers, social workers and other professionals to work together to put in place appropriate teaching and learning strategies, ensure access to services and

The virtual school head

Building on the good practice of some local authorities, we are piloting a 'virtual school head' in 11 local authority areas.

Virtual school heads will oversee the education of children in care in their authority, and those children in the authority's care who are placed out of authority, as if they were the head of a single school. They will work both across the local authority and its children's trust partners and with individual schools, including Academies, and FE settings that are providing 14-19 education for children in care. Acting as a source of expertise, offering capacity to broker arrangements that are likely to improve outcomes for children in care, virtual school heads will work with School Improvement Partners, school headteachers and designated teachers to raise the attainment of children in care, reduce absence and tackle exclusions, and ensure that provision meets their learning needs.

Virtual school heads will champion the educational needs of children in care, spreading best practice across schools, the authority and its partners. In particular they will improve working between education and social care. They will report to the local authority's Director of Children's Services and Lead Member for Children's Services on the improvements that need to be made. This is an important element of the corporate parenting role.

In the exceptional circumstances that children are placed out of authority, the virtual school head should develop good links with those authorities to enable them to champion the education of those children placed out of authority.

We will extend the role of the virtual school head to all local authorities, setting out a role based on the lessons learnt from these pilots.

support and minimise disruption to a child or young person's education.

4.33 The involvement of a teacher in the design and delivery of PEPs is crucial to ensuring it meets children and young people's learning needs, that appropriate teaching and learning strategies are identified and that it is implemented by the school. Whilst some teachers fulfil this role very well, feedback indicates that schools do not always take an active role in planning and implementing PEPs and that some social workers do not sufficiently involve schools in the care planning process. As a result PEPs do not always reflect the child or young person's needs, are not kept up to date and are not effectively implemented. In order to address this, we will:

- **Publish revised Children Act Guidance in 2009 setting out the role that designated teachers, social workers, carers and children and young people themselves should take in designing and delivering PEPs**. In addition, as part of their role in driving up the attainment of children in care, virtual school heads will take an overview of the local authority's PEP process, helping to ensure that they are of high quality, are effectively implemented and regularly reviewed.

Education in children's homes

4.34 Local authorities are under a duty to arrange appropriate provision of education. For the majority of children this will be a full-time place in a local mainstream school unless the circumstances of the child – such as particular special educational needs – mean this is unsuitable.

4.35 A small minority of children and young people receive their education in residential children's homes. Local authorities must ensure that they arrange provision based on the needs of children and young people, not on convenience of the placement. For some children education in a children's home will be the right choice; however there are also concerns over the quality of education being offered in some children's homes.

4.36 Chapter 3 sets out the measures that we are taking to improve the outcomes for children and young people placed in children's homes. In addition, we will explore with Ofsted how best to assess provision to ensure that children's homes providing education meet the high standards necessary for children in care.

Personalised learning

4.37 Over £1 billion has been committed to personalised learning across the country, weighted toward areas with low prior attainment and high deprivation. This investment is designed, in particular, to support small group and one to one intervention for children who have fallen behind in English and Maths and need help to catch up, and to help learners from deprived backgrounds access after school and year-round activities. Personalised learning will have a particular impact on children in care who are not reaching expected standards of learning.

4.38 The publication in January 2007 of the report of the *Teaching and Learning in 2020 Review*[7] has developed our understanding of personalised learning and how it can help all children progress, achieve and participate, and reduce attainment gaps between under-performing children and their peers. The report's analysis and recommendations will inform our long term strategy for improving teaching and learning through this Comprehensive Spending Review period and beyond.

4.39 Each school will develop its own plans for personalised learning, sensitive to the needs and circumstances of the children it serves[8]. By 2008 every school will have access to leading teachers in intervention in English and Maths and a leading teacher in gifted and talented provision. Our expectation is that these will form part of a team of teachers who will work together to identify the range of interventions needed to support children in the school and help teachers to plan ways to use these to support individual children, including children in care.

4.40 Leading teachers for intervention are expected to monitor the progress of underperforming pupils and ensure that each pupil is receiving the right kind of intervention to enable them to catch up in core subjects. They will identify where intervention is not sufficient to improve the attainment and engagement of particular pupils or groups of pupils, and make links to additional support. For children in care this will mean working closely with the designated teacher and virtual school head to identify the additional support available to children in care, augmenting the focused teaching they will be receiving in core subjects.

4.41 We announced in the 2007 Budget that we would fund schools to ensure that by 2011 every pupil should have access to a single member of staff – for example a learning guide, a class teacher, a form tutor or a Director of Studies – who is able to coordinate a package of support that best helps that pupil[9]. There will be a range of ways of delivering this support. The best approach will depend on a school's existing staff structure and learning and pastoral support systems. For some children in care this will be the designated teacher. In other schools, with larger numbers of children in care, the adult undertaking this role should be familiar with their PEP and should

7   *2020 Vision: Report of the Teaching and Learning in 2020 Review Group*, Department for Education and Skills (2007).

8   See: *Budget 2007, Building Britain's long-term future: Prosperity and fairness for families*, HM Treasury (2007). For www.standards.dfes.gov.uk/personalised learning

9   See: *Budget 2007, Building Britain's long-term future: Prosperity and fairness for families*, HM Treasury, (2007).

work closely with the designated teacher, who should take oversight of their provision and maintain close links with the child's social worker.

Personal educational allowance

4.42 To help meet the additional educational needs of children in care, *Care Matters* proposed a £500 personalised education allowance. Following support from the consultation, **from 2008 we will provide £500 a year for each child in care who is at risk of not reaching the expected standards of attainment to support their educational and developmental needs**.

4.43 We will set out how local authorities will be expected to use the £500. This entitlement must not replace the services that schools, local authorities and carers already provide. It will provide support for a wide range of additional activities that support the educational development of the child or young person. It will give children in care greater access to extended services, personal tuition outside school, positive activities, and trips and visits that will enrich their learning and support their development.

4.44 This additional resource will be used to support the aims set out in the child or young person's personal education plan. Overall allocation will be overseen by the virtual school head, or where one is not yet in place, a senior manager in the local authority responsible for the education of children in care. However,

children and young people's wishes and feelings should be taken into account in the allocation of funding. At an individual level, plans for use of the £500 will be agreed by the designated teacher, the social worker, the child or young person and their carer, as part of the discussion of their overall personal education plan and care plan.

Progression

4.45 Increased resources are enabling schools to focus on the progression of individual pupils. As a result teachers are now better able to meet the individual needs of children and young people in care. To help schools develop approaches to personalised learning and progression the Department for Education and Skills launched the *Making Good Progress* pilot. This will trial new ways to measure, assess, report and stimulate pupils' progress in school, focusing on the needs of low attaining pupils, including children and young people in care. It will start in 483 schools in 10 local authorities in September 2007.

4.46 Focused at Key Stages 2 and 3, the pilot will comprise four measures:

- **Assessment for progression:** single-level tests to improve the pace of progression; and better use of periodic assessment to track the progress of individual pupils;

- **One to one tuition:** providing pupils with up to 10 hours of target tuition in English and/or Maths;

- **Progression targets:** exploring how best to formulate measures and set targets for improved pupil progression; and

- **Progression premium:** a school level incentive payment related to the school's actual success for securing better rates of progression for their under attaining pupils.

4.47 108,000 pupils will take part in the pilot, with 43,000 being offered up to 10 hours of targeted tuition in English and/or Maths. Tuition will be designed to meet children and young people's individual needs, and delivered at the exact time of need. It will be focused on pupils who are behind national expectations, are falling behind, or are in care.

4.48 **Supporting this, HSBC are providing £1 million to support individual tutoring for children in care. This provision will be overseen by a virtual school head in four local authority areas. We estimate that it will give up to 1000 children in care access to approximately 15 hours of tutoring a year based on their educational needs.**

Gifted and talented children in care

4.49 All schools should support their gifted and talented learners – around 10 per cent of the pupil population, identified on the basis of ability as well as attainment or performance. We believe that more children and young people in care should be identified as gifted and talented. However, analysis of the 2006 school census shows that children in care are currently under-represented in the cohorts of students identified as gifted and talented.

4.50 From September 2007 the gifted and talented programme will reach and support more learners, and there will be a stronger focus on those who have potential that they are not realising due to disadvantage, including children in care. Under the new Young, Gifted and Talented programme, all identified gifted and talented learners will automatically become members of the Gifted and Talented Learner Academy. We have also set up an 'Excellence Hub' in each region to provide additional opportunities in school holidays and outside school hours. In both cases, additional support will be available to learners from disadvantaged backgrounds, including children in care.

4.51 Working with the appointed Gifted and Talented Leading Teacher, the designated teacher will play a central role in supporting gifted and talented children in care and in encouraging their schools to ensure that their talents are identified. We will:

- **Set out in guidance on the role of the designated teacher how they should consider gifted and talented provision and work with the leading teacher for gifted and talented pupils.**

4.52 Children of secondary school age will remain a member of the Gifted and Talented Learner Academy even when they move schools. This membership will provide continuity of provision for gifted and talented children in care, providing an element of stability in their education and challenging the stigma and low expectations that are often associated with this group.

Special Educational Needs

4.53 28% of children in care have a statement of special educational needs (SEN), compared with 3% of all children[10]. For some children in care, meeting these additional needs is a vital part of ensuring that they receive a high quality education. Designated teachers should work with the special educational needs coordinator to ensure that additional needs are identified and addressed through the child or young person's PEP.

4.54 The Government's long term SEN strategy *Removing Barriers to Achievement*[11] and *Aiming High for Disabled Children* set out how we are improving services for children with SEN or a disability. Due to the additional barrier to learning that they face, the virtual school head will take a central role in ensuring that children in care with SEN or a disability have adequate provision to meet their needs. The virtual school head will work across the local authority, and its children's trust partners, and with individual schools to champion the needs of children in care with SEN or disabilities to help ensure that the necessary support is provided.

4.55 For some, appealing to a SEN and disability tribunal (SENDIST) can be problematic. Whilst foster carers can appeal to the tribunal, children in care do not have someone with the same degree of independence from the local authority as a birth parent in a position to appeal on their behalf. We will:

● **Issue strengthened guidance to carers and those with parental responsibility setting out how they can support children in care with SEN, including their right to appeal.** Where carers experience difficulty supporting a child or young person's appeal we will ensure that Independent Reviewing Officers (IROs) advise those who appeal to SENDIST on behalf of children in care.

4.56 In response to the Education and Select Committee's report on SEN, Ofsted are undertaking a study in 2009/10 to review progress in improving SEN provision. **We have also asked Ofsted to report on the progress of children in care with SEN as part of their 2009/10 work programme.** In light of their report, we will consider whether the present framework for SEN, including the arrangements for appeal to SENDIST on behalf of children in care, should be reviewed.

---

10 *Statistics in Education, Outcome Indicators for Looked After Children, Twelve months to 30 September 2006, England,* Statistical First Release Office of National Statistics (2007).

11 Removing barriers to achievement: the Government's strategy for SEN, DfES (2004).

Extended activities

4.57 Evidence[12] shows that extended services help raise children and young people's educational attainment and social and emotional skills. This can be of particular benefit for children in care who may need additional support to boost their learning and social and emotional development.

4.58 There are currently over 5,000 extended schools offering access to a wide range of activities comprising: 8am-6pm year round childcare (primary schools only); study support; parenting support and family learning; swift and easy referral to targeted and specialist services and community access to schools facilities, including adult learning. By 2010 every school will be an extended school, enabling all children in care to benefit.

4.59 We are committed to ensuring access to extended activities for all pupils, including the most deprived. *Aiming higher for children: supporting families*[13] announced **£217 million by 2010-11 to offer two hours of free extended activities a week during term time, with two weeks a year of part-time provision, for pupils eligible for free school meals. We will also make this offer available for children in care.** Children in care who are at risk of not reaching expected standards in their education will be also able to access further provision through their £500 personalised education allowance.

14–19 provision

4.60 14-19 reform is creating new, flexible, routes to learning in both school and further education (FE) colleges, which increase the access to learning for children in care. Every 14-19 year old will have: the opportunity to master the basics; better and more engaging curriculum choices; highly-valued qualifications that recognise their talents and ensure they are learning the things they need to learn; and more stretching learning routes that enable progression. These reforms will be particularly beneficial to children in care who have fallen behind in their learning or have missed out on education.

4.61 By September 2013, a new statutory entitlement will ensure that every 14-19 year old in the country will have the choice between 14 types of Diploma, whether they are preparing for the most demanding university courses, planning to enter the workforce directly at 18, or are currently not engaged in education or training. The first five Diplomas will be taught from September 2008, and a further five from September 2009.

4.62 Alongside this we are developing new functional skills qualifications – embedding them within GCSEs in English, Maths and ICT and making them an integral part of Diplomas and Apprenticeships – and a more coherent set of entry level and level 1 qualifications. These will ensure that

---

12 See for example: *Cummings, Dyson et al (2005, 2006 and forthcoming), Evaluation of full service extended schools, DfES Research Reports and Extended services in schools and children's centres*, Ofsted (2006), HMI 2609.

13 *Aiming High for Children: Supporting Families*, HM Treasury and DfES (2007)

children in care can develop the skills they need for further education and employment, as well as being able to progress more readily up the qualifications ladder. To support children in care better we are including information on the needs of children in care in the FE *Principals Qualifying Programme*, which will be rolled out nationally from September 2007, and we are piloting an approach to helping FE providers develop pastoral support for children in care and care leavers.

4.63 These reforms will increase the number of learning routes available to children in care, allowing individuals greater flexibility about what, where, and how they study. As part of their PEP (or post 16 their Care Pathway Plan) young people in care should identify appropriate 14 – 19 learning. Social workers and carers have an important role in providing advice and guidance to young people in care in order to raise aspirations, widen horizons and increase their understanding of what is available.

4.64 However, some children in care will require extra guidance and support. Through the reforms set out in *Youth Matters*, we are creating a system of Targeted Youth Support (TYS) that provides integrated support to children and young people who are experiencing barriers to participation in learning. All local areas will have developed TYS arrangements by 2008. For children in care, social workers form an important part of these arrangements, often acting as their lead professional. As we implement TYS we will work with the Training and Development Agency for Schools (TDA) to ensure that the support provided to local areas to develop their arrangements helps to involve social workers in the new structures and ensure children in care are given the support that they need to progress their learning.

4.65 High quality information, advice and guidance (IAG) forms an important part of this support, enabling children in care to decide what to study and understand what impact different choices might have on their future. This will include helping young people to experience the range of options before they have to make a choice. In summer 2007 we will publish new national quality standards for the IAG that all young people should receive. From April 2008 local authorities, working through children's trusts, will be responsible for the funding and commissioning of services that will deliver IAG in accordance with the standards – paying particular regard to the needs of vulnerable groups such as children in care.

Raising Expectations: staying on in education and training

4.66 The *Raising Expectations: Staying in Education and Training Post-16* Green Paper set out our intention to raise the participation age of young people in education or training to 17 in 2013, and 18 in 2015. We do not expect all young people to remain in the classroom. Young people can participate in education or training in school, in a FE college, or at work. All forms of valuable learning, including the learning undertaken by young people within work, which prepares young people for life, will be recognised. Support for children in care will be set out later this year in the Government's response to the consultation on *Raising Expectations*.

4.67 Where young people aged 16 to 18 are in employment, we will expect that they will undertake accredited training that leads to recognised qualifications, as these will give them a good basis for further progression in employment and further learning. These changes will give children in care a much richer set of opportunities to further their education. However, it is important that we ensure that young people in care are given the necessary support and guidance as they continue their education.

4.68 Chapter 6 sets out how we will pilot giving young people a much stronger voice over when they move on to independence – through 'Right 2Be Cared4' – and we will extend the entitlement to the support of a personal advisor up to the age of 25 for all care leavers who are either in education or wish to return to education.

Attendance and exclusions:

4.69 Data show that in 2005/6 13% of children in care missed 25 or more days of education and 0.8% of children in care were permanently excluded compared to 0.1% of all children[14]. Despite efforts to improve the education of children in care, these figures have remained largely unchanged: In 2004/5 these figures were 13% and 0.9% respectively.

4.70 Poor attendance has a dramatic impact on outcomes for children in care. Being out of school can impact more on this group of children and young people than others; school can be the only source of stability in their lives. Research indicates that children and young people with high rates of absence are significantly less likely to obtain 5 good GCSEs than students with good attendance records[15].

4.71 Much more needs to be done to improve the attendance of children in care and reduce the need for exclusion. Local authorities, schools, social workers and carers all share the responsibility for improving the attendance and reducing exclusions of children in care. Tackling this will provide a firm foundation for improving their educational attainment.

4.72 An important step is improving our understanding of why children in care experience higher levels of absence and exclusions. **We will ask Ofsted to conduct a thematic review in 2008/09 of schools' practice in relation to the exclusion of children in care. In addition we will commission further research on why**

---

14 *Statistics in Education, Outcome Indicators for Looked After Children, Twelve months to 30 September 2006,* Statistical First Release. England. Office of National Statistics. (2007)

15 Morris & Rutt (2005), *An analysis of pupil attendance data in Excellence in Cities (EiC) areas and non-EiC EAZs: Final report,* DfES Research Report 657

children in care have higher levels of absence and exclusion and how this can be reduced. The lessons learnt will inform the work of the Primary and Secondary National Strategies.

School and local authority provision

4.73 Improvements in pupil level data have enabled the National Strategies behaviour and attendance field forces to concentrate their work on the individual pupils and schools with high levels of absence. The National Strategies field forces provide focused support and challenge to schools and local authorities and introduce effective ways of reducing poor attendance and behaviour.

4.74 Improved pupil level data on children in care will be available later in 2007. We will:

- **Ask the National Strategies behaviour and attendance field forces to work with target local authorities and schools to tackle high rates of absence amongst looked after children, including challenging local authority performance through their termly regional network meetings.**

4.75 Where an exclusion is absolutely necessary it is crucial that schools and local authorities have first considered the additional needs of children in care and assessed what additional support can be provided. No child in care should be excluded from a school without discussion with the local authority to ensure that there is suitable alternative provision available elsewhere. In summer 2007 we will:

- **Publish revised statutory guidance on exclusions, which will come into force for all schools, including Academies, in September 2007. This will set out that children in care must only be excluded as a last resort and that, in conjunction with the local authority, schools should first consider alternative options for supporting the child or young person.**

4.76 We have recently enhanced the expectations regarding educational provision for excluded pupils. From September 2007 where a pupil is permanently excluded local authorities will be responsible for ensuring appropriate provision is available from day six of the exclusion. For fixed period exclusions this responsibility lies with the school. Further to this, we will:

- **Set out our view in the forthcoming revised guidance that provision should be arranged from the first day of an exclusion of a child in care to ensure that they do not suffer from a break in their education.**

4.77 Schools should work together to improve the provision for children in care. From September 2007 we expect all secondary schools to be working in local partnerships to improve behaviour and tackle persistent absence, reduce the need for exclusion and agree strategies for educating 'hard to place pupils'. Schools already working in this way have demonstrated that such partnerships are effective ways of tackling the need for exclusion and reducing persistent absence. We will:

- **Ask all schools and local authorities to monitor absence and exclusion of children in care and put in place strategies for improving the attendance and reducing exclusions of children in care.** These protocols will often be most effectively delivered through working in partnership with other schools.

4.78 School behaviour and attendance partnerships will be supported by local authority virtual school heads. Like a conventional head teacher, virtual school heads for children in care will play a central role in improving the attendance and reducing the number of exclusions of children in care in their 'school'.

4.79 As part of their role, **virtual school heads should be held accountable by Directors of Children's Services for improving the attendance, behaviour and rates of exclusion of children and young people in care** and, through school improvement partners (SIPs), should support and challenge schools with high levels of absence or exclusion amongst the children in care population.

4.80 Children and young people told us that they want to see local authorities held to account for improving attendance and reducing exclusions in the same way as parents are. Local authorities and schools must take responsibility for reducing absence and exclusions of children in care. Practice across the services of the children's trust must support children and young people in care to access a high quality education.

4.81 As part of the revised Children Act 1989 guidance we will review care planning procedures to ensure that local authority care planning decisions do not adversely impact on the education

Gloucestershire protocol for children in care at risk of exclusion

There are around 400 children in care in Gloucestershire. The county council are piloting a protocol with all of their schools to reduce the impact of exclusion on this vulnerable group.

When exclusion is necessary, Gloucestershire aspires to make provision from day one rather than day six. Instead of excluding pupils, head teachers are asked to contact the Looked After Children team or Gloucestershire Reintegration Service who will arrange a temporary managed transfer to a Pupil Reintegration Centre (PRC). Staff will assess the child's needs and arrange appropriate local provision for a short period up to six weeks after which the child returns to school. On occasions a permanent transfer to another school may be best for the child. In one case a school was struggling to keep a child in care in school and arranged for the child to be moved to a reintegration centre for assessment. The child's attendance has improved dramatically and they have successfully returned to school.

of children in care, including their attendance at school. Where local authorities have not provided a school place for children in care or are not supporting their attendance, children and young people can complain through the complaints procedure outlined in Chapter 7.

4.82 Local authorities will be held to account for improving outcomes for children in care through a three year programme of proportionate inspection led by Ofsted. Because of the central importance of attendance and permanent exclusion to improving the education of children in care, we will ask Ofsted to ensure that local authorities are held accountable for rates of attendance and permanent exclusion as part of that inspection.

4.83 Those with responsibility for the day-to-day care of the child, including those working in children's homes, have a vital role to play in improving attendance and reducing the need for exclusion, by supporting children in care in their learning. *Care Matters* consultation responses indicated that at present some children's homes do not fulfil their responsibility towards the education of children in care, in particular with regard to school attendance. Children and young people said that children's homes do not take their education seriously enough.

4.84 The national minimum standards for children's homes are currently being reviewed. As part of this review we will:

● **Update the standards to ensure that children's homes take action to improve attendance and reduce the need for exclusion.** To support this, we are strengthening the enforcement options available to Ofsted to raise standards in children's homes by ensuring better compliance with the National Minimum Standards.

Supporting carers

4.85 Like parents, carers are a crucial influence on what children and young people in care experience and achieve. Evidence shows that what parents and carers do has one of the biggest impacts on the education of children and young people but far too many children in care still fail to reach their potential. Carers have a critical role in instilling values and aspirations, and supporting the development of wider interpersonal and social skills, which are central to raising attainment.

4.86 In March 2007 we published *Every Parent Matters*, setting out the range of support and advice that is available to parents and carers and a vision for how they can shape the services available to them. Raising attainment for children in care relies on carers having access to good information and services, which enable them to play an active part in the school and wider life of children and young people. Providers should pay particular attention to ensuring that information and services are accessed by those supporting children in care and that they are appropriate to their needs.

4.87 As they develop support for parents and carers – including access to parenting programmes through Sure Start Children's Centres and extended schools, expanding the role of Children's Information Services and asking services to develop approaches to engaging parents and carers such as Parent Councils – local authorities and individual services must ensure that they meet the needs of carers. We are developing a number of approaches to support foster carers and children and young people's birth parents. These include:

- **Improved help for carers to support literacy:** Children in care face particular challenges in literacy. Working with BAAF, the Maudsley hospital and the London Borough of Southwark, we are developing a programme to provide training for carers to help them to support their children better as they acquire skills, including primary level literacy skills; and

- **Better information for carers:** New technology can used to provide on-line teaching and hold the school work and records of a child in care together in one place. On-line support can help with revision, coursework or homework and record storage can allow new schools, carers or children in care easy to

access information, such as a personal education plan or attendance data.

4.88 Like any parent, carers and social workers should engage children and young people in learning: support them with their homework, attend school parent's evenings and help make appropriate choices for their education. It is vital that carers develop good links with schools as this is central to ensuring that they understand the educational needs of children in care. However, carers can have trouble knowing how to approach schools on their child's behalf[16]. It is, therefore, equally important that schools reach out to carers, and identify the barriers that they may face in engaging with the school.

4.89 In 2004, we published *Who does what: How social workers and carers can support the education of looked after children.*[17] This document provides information for carers to help them support the education of young people in care, from the early years to the time they leave care. On entering school, Home-School Agreements provide information about the agreed responsibilities of schools and parents and what is expected of pupils. We will:

- **Strengthen Home-School Agreements, making sure that schools are using them effectively, and are giving particular**

---

16 Comfort RL (2007), *For the Love of Learning: Promoting educational achievement for looked after and adopted children*, Adoption and Fostering Volume 31, Number 1, Special Issue: Education, Jackson S (ed), BAFF.

17 Available to download at: www.dfes.gov.uk/educationprotects

consideration to foster carers and residential care workers.

4.90 Alongside better information, we are improving the support available to foster carers. The new Children's Workforce Development Council standards for foster carers include details of how they support the education of children in care. We are currently reviewing the National Minimum Standards (NMS) for fostering services and children's homes and will be consulting on them following legislative changes set out in this White Paper. **As part of the NMS review we will ensure that an emphasis is placed on supporting the education of children in care.**

Increased accountability

4.91 Delivery of a first class education requires responsibility for improving

---

Support for Carers

Fred is a year 9 student. He has lived with his current foster carers for four and a half years. Throughout this period Fred and his foster carers have had the following home support from the Calderdale Looked After Children Education Service (LACES), on top of personalised support received at school:

- literacy support in school and at home from the LACES literacy teacher;

- year 9 SATS support in school and at home from the literacy teacher;

- a LACES "buddy", supporting the transition from junior school, including half termly visits in school reinforced by home visits to troubleshoot difficulties and encourage Fred and his foster carers;

- attendance tracking by the LACES education welfare officer, to ensure problems are picked up early before they become established;

- weekly attendance at an out of school leisure club for children in care. Fred has attended over 200 sessions including residential visits, breaking world records, circus skills, swimming and raising money for charity; and

- free passport to leisure and 'maxcards' giving free and discounted entry into local and regional attractions.

Fred's foster carers value this practical support and feel it is integral to placement stability. It has helped keep them involved in Fred's education, the links with the school help them to get their voices heard, and the out of school hours support provides structured respite for them and an outlet for Fred's talents. They feel that this support is "not just meetings but is of practical value and deals with his issues at hand".

As a result Fred's education is on track and his placement is stable despite continuing disruptions in contact with his birth family.

outcomes for children in care throughout the system – from individual teachers, from head teachers and schools, from social workers, and from the local authority and their children's trust partners.

School level accountability

4.92 Improved educational outcomes for children in care will be a specific measure against which the Government will judge the success of its efforts to raise attainment and narrow achievement gaps. This is a national challenge in which every school to should play its part. To help develop solutions that make a difference to the specific needs of children in care, head teachers and their designated teachers will be supported by a virtual school head.

4.93 Since September 2005 schools have been inspected against their contribution to the five Every Child Matters outcomes: Be Healthy, Stay Safe, Enjoy and Achieve, Make a Positive Contribution, and Achieve Economic Well-Being. Schools are expected to evaluate and report on their provision for children in care as part of their school self evaluation. School Improvement Partners should discuss the progress of children in care with the school. The support of the virtual school head will help schools to demonstrate how they are supporting children in care. In addition we will:

- **Provide training for school governors to help them to**

understand the needs of children in care and effectively hold the school to account.

Local authority accountability

4.94 As the corporate parent, local authorities must take the lead in ensuring that children in care receive a high quality education. Revised Children Act 1989 guidance will set out how local authorities should meet their duty to improve the education of children in care.

4.95 Local authorities are required to set annual targets relating to the education of children in care, helping to ensure that all local authorities place a priority on raising the attainment of children in care. As set out in the Local Government White Paper, *Strong and Prosperous Communities*, from 2008 local authorities will continue to set statutory education targets as part of their Local Area Agreements (LAAs). Our aim is that this will include targets on the education of children in care. We will issue guidance on the new round of statutory target setting by the end of summer 2007.

4.96 The virtual school head, or equivalent interim senior manager, will report to the Director of Children's Services and Lead Member for Children's Services setting out where the local authority, and their partners, needs to improve their provision for the education of children in care. Where children and young people are placed out of authority, (see Chapter 3), the virtual school head should develop good links with the senior management of those authorities to enable them to raise the standards of education for those children.

4.97 Sharing practice between virtual school heads and authorities will play a vital role in developing effective ways of improving the education of children in care. In 2000 we launched the 'Education Protects' network. Each region has an education protects facilitator to embed best practice amongst local authorities. As local authorities develop their virtual school heads, **we will work with the Government Offices to develop these networks to share good practice**, linked to the Annual Stocktake on outcomes for children in care.

4.98 Following the completion of the programme of joint area reviews, alongside risk-based inspection of local authorities, **Ofsted's programme of proportionate inspection of services for children in care will include judging whether their education is being improved.**

Chapter 5
Promoting health and wellbeing

"What health means to me? Running and playing; being with my friends; on my bike and exercise; eating food, fruit; sleeping at night and good dreams."

Young person

Summary

Securing the health and wider wellbeing of children and young people in care is of fundamental importance. Good health makes an active and enjoyable life possible, as well as underpinning achievement in school and the work place.

This chapter sets out a strong package of measures to support health and wider wellbeing. In doing so, it addresses concerns voiced through the *Care Matters* Green Paper consultation that our proposals for improving the health of children in care were not sufficiently robust. By building on and strengthening the Green Paper proposals, we now believe that a significant improvement in health-related outcomes is possible. Our measures include:

- A range of mechanisms through which health delivery partners can better promote the health of children in care;

- A focus on children in care in the Joint Strategic Needs Assessment;

- A number of measures to transform the potential of children and young people's leisure time;

- Providing practical support and guidance to help children in care participate in positive leisure time activities; and

- Clear roles and responsibilities for promoting the health and wellbeing of children in care.

Introduction

5.1 The physical and mental health of children and young people in care is too often poor in comparison to that of their peers. Children in care have higher rates of substance misuse and teenage pregnancy than those in the non-care population and a much greater prevalence of mental health problems.

5.2 There are strong connections between poverty and poor health and these inequalities will already have impacted on many children in care. For some children, however, this will be combined with early experience of trauma and abuse which will require specific interventions in order to address the harm effectively. It is important that these therapeutic interventions use an evidence-based approach which includes the child's carers as part of the recovery model.

5.3 Although these inequalities are well known, the solutions to addressing them are not straightforward and do not lie entirely with health services. Secure attachments and friendships, healthy eating, the pursuit of hobbies, access to sporting and other positive activities and avoidance of risky behaviours are all important preventive factors that make a major contribution to a holistic and integrated approach to health.

5.4 Health care bodies do, however, have a clear role in ensuring the timely and effective delivery of health services to children in care. To help them do so, it is important that the right opportunities and incentives are in place, and that they are able to work in partnership with the local authority to address jointly the health needs of children in care.

Promoting the health of children in care

5.5 The actions of local authorities and healthcare bodies in addressing the health of children in care are currently informed by *The National Service Framework for Children, Young People, and Maternity Services*, Department of Health (2004) and *Promoting the Health of Looked After Children*, Department of Health (2002)[1]. This second document sets out the roles and responsibilities regarding children in care, while also addressing key issues such as health assessment and planning, and health promotion. Currently *Promoting the Health of Looked After Children* holds statutory status amongst local authorities but is non-statutory for the NHS. In order to better promote joint working and to remove any inconsistency in the application of the guidance, we will:

- **Re-issue this guidance in 2008 on a statutory footing for both local authorities and healthcare bodies.** For local authorities this will form part of the revised Children Act 1989 guidance.

- **Use the statutory guidance to strengthen protocols and agreements with NHS bodies and update regulations as necessary; and**

- **Address the need for co-ordination within healthcare**

---

1   We also will work in partnership with the Department of Health, the National Institute for Health and Clinical Excellence (NICE) and others, to explore the scope for developing new NICE guidance on the health of children in care.

bodies to meet the needs of children in care.

5.6 In doing so we will also update its content to:

- **Set out expectations surrounding the health assessments of children in care and the subsequent health plan.**

5.7 The guidance will also include the need to address substance misuse. Evidence suggests that children in care are four times more likely than their peers to smoke, use alcohol and misuse drugs. Addressing the early onset of substance misuse and the underlying causes can prevent problems escalating.

5.8 Early identification and assessment of substance misuse should take place within the context of the assessment of the young person's overall needs and not as a stand alone activity. Most of the time, this can be provided by the carers and professionals who are already known to the young person. In some cases there will be a need for more specialist substance misuse interventions by specialist workers.

5.9 This expectation is not new. Assessment of substance misuse already forms a part of the child's (or young person's) annual assessment within the Integrated Children's System Framework. Inclusion in statutory guidance will, however, ensure consistency of approach.

5.10 Although the designated doctor and nurse roles set out in *Promoting the Health of Looked After Children* are working well, they are not designed to improve co-ordination of health services for individual children in care, or progress actions against the child's health care plan. Too often these tasks fall to the social worker operating outside of the NHS. We believe that there is a need to address these difficulties.

5.11 Subject to Comprehensive Spending Review outcomes, we will **explore how best to improve co-ordination, including the potential benefits of a named health professional.**

General Practice

5.12 When children in care are moved, the time taken to receive their general practice record once it is requested can be anything from a few weeks to a few months. As a result, the new practice often does not have the benefit of the old record when the child attends the first consultation.

5.13 Following national trials, development of roll-out plans are underway for GP2GP – the NHS Connecting for Health project. This will enable all patients' Electronic Health records to be transferred instantaneously between the 9000 GP practices in England. As a result GPs and their teams will be able to provide children in care with a safer and more efficient service.

2   We will also publish guidance on improving the outcomes for teenage parents, which will set out associated expectations for young parents in the care population.

The named health professional may be responsible for:

- ensuring that the child's health assessments and reviews are undertaken;

- co-ordinating the child's health care plan on actions falling to the NHS to ensure they are undertaken and tracked and any blockages are sorted;

- acting as a contact point for the child, carer and other health practitioners about the child's health needs;

- acting as a key health contact for the child's social worker;

- holding the health chronology for the child;

- interpreting health needs to social services and education;

- ensuring that when a child is moved out of the PCT area, records are swiftly transferred and critical information about the child is made available to health professionals in the child's new area of residence;

- ensuring the particular needs of disabled children, including those with complex healthcare needs, are taken into account; and

- acting as a local point of contact for the responsible commissioner for children placed out of the original PCT area.

Understanding health needs

5.14 More broadly, healthcare bodies and local authorities will need to ensure that they understand the health needs of children in care and use joint planning arrangements within children's trusts to address them.

5.15 Key to this process will be the Joint Strategic Needs Assessment (JSNA) which, subject to Parliamentary approval, will be made statutory by the Local Government and Public Involvement in Health Bill. The JSNA will be carried out by councils and PCTs, and will strengthen their ability to identify the needs of vulnerable groups including children in care and those at risk of being taken into care.

5.16 The JSNA will draw on and align with the assessment made for the Children

and Young People's Plan and will support the development of the Sustainable Community Strategy. It will also provide a basis for the selection of targets within Local Area Agreements (LAA) and underpin the delivery of improved commissioning for health and wellbeing. We will:

- **Make clear in statutory guidance on the JSNA that local areas should consider any relevant information on children in care when making the assessment;**

- **Include relevant data sources for children in care in guidance on information to support the JSNA; and**

- **Conduct a review of JSNAs following their commencement to ensure that they are effective in**

addressing the needs of vulnerable groups such as children in care.

Promoting positive mental health for children in care

5.17 One of the factors likely to emerge in the JSNA will be the mental health of children and young people in care. Foster carers frequently report that the most common difficulty experienced by the children and young people they care for is their emotional wellbeing and mental health. In some areas, significant numbers of unaccompanied asylum seeking children may also present additional specific and complex needs resulting from past experiences in their country of origin.

5.18 Despite evidence of the prevalence of clinical mental health difficulties amongst children in care[3], many children's trusts fail to provide children and young people with the access to Child and Adolescent Mental Health Services (CAMHS) that they and their carers feel they need.

5.19 To improve the level of CAMHS provision available to children and young people the Government increased direct CAMHS investment by over £300m during the three years to 2006, £86m in 2006/07 and £88m in 2007/08. It has also encouraged the maintenance of dedicated children in care CAMHS services. The case for such provision is strong. By focusing on a specific high need group, CAMHS services are able to adopt a preventive approach and to work with, and through, a wide body of people capable of supporting the child or young person.

5.20 Despite significant recent improvements in CAMHS services, we know that more needs to be done and that in some areas the mental health

Aldine House Secure Children's Home – supported by **Sheffield Forensic Child and Adolescent Mental Health Services (CAMHS)** – has taken a holistic approach to securing emotional health and wellbeing for its residents. Its approach combines building staff capacity through a 3-day emotional health training course and a bereavement and loss module, with access to positive activities such as Duke of Edinburgh award scheme. Their aim is to enrol all young people into the scheme on admission.

Aldine House also supports young people to develop skills for employment and seeks to provide progression routes into work. An example of this is the relationship with a local hospice which has enabled one young woman to produce artwork for the hospice to sell. Links have also been made with local employment agencies and Connexions in Sheffield.

---

3   The Department of Health commissioned the Office of National Statistics to carry out a survey on the 'Mental health of young people looked after by local authorities in England.' This was published in 2002 and confirmed findings of earlier research about the high level of mental health need amongst looked after children, particularly those in residential care: 45% were assessed as having a mental health disorder (compared with around 10% of the general population); 37% had conduct disorders, 12% emotional disorders & 7% as hyperactive; 75% of children in residential care were assessed as having a mental health disorder

needs of children in care are simply not being prioritised adequately within health care planning. We will:

- **Use statutory guidance to ensure CAMHS provide targeted and dedicated provision that appropriately prioritises children in care.**

5.21 The LAA also provides a major opportunity for local authorities and their partners to increase the focus on CAMHS services and to promote the mental health of children in care more broadly.

5.22 As part of the reforms set out in the White Paper *Strong and Prosperous Communities* the Government is currently developing a National Indicator Set which will inform future performance management arrangements and set the framework for LAA improvement targets.

5.23 The indicators in the national set will be reported upon annually. Where an indicator shows outcomes to be unacceptably poor, a related improvement target may need to be adopted. In those circumstances, each member of the local strategic partnership – including the PCT – would be under a statutory duty both to agree and to have regard to the target.

5.24 We will:

- **Consider how best to ensure that the mental health of children in care is reflected in future local authority performance management arrangements. In doing so, we will explore the case for developing new indicators focused on the psychological and emotional health and wellbeing of children, and specifically on the emotional and behavioural difficulties of children in care.**

Promoting sexual health

5.25 Evidence shows that children in care often have poor sexual health and may be more vulnerable to involvement in risky sexual activity, exploitative and abusive relationships, and early parenthood. Children's trusts will therefore need to ensure that children and young people in care have effective sex and relationship education (SRE) and easy access to specialist services as required[4].

5.26 School is a key source of SRE for young people and all schools should provide all pupils with a comprehensive programme of SRE within Personal Social and Health Education (PSHE). This should:

- reflect the Sex and Relationships Guidance, DfES (2000). As part of gaining Healthy Schools status, schools must assess all pupils' progress and achievement in line with this guidance. All schools should be participating in the Healthy Schools Programme by 2009;

- be planned and evaluated against the Qualifications and Curriculum

---

4   *Teenage Pregnancy Next Steps*, DfES (2006) sets out what all local authorities and PCTs should have in place to accelerate reductions in under 18 conception rates, drawn from high performing areas. This highlights the importance of targeted prevention work with young people in care and those leaving care.

Authority end of key stage statements for PSHE (2005); and

- be delivered by specialist teams – made up of trained teachers, school and community nurses, voluntary sector partners and other relevant professionals.

5.27 Unfortunately some children and young people in care experience interruptions and gaps in education that may lead to them missing SRE in schools. Others may also have an additional need for information, advice and support beyond that of their peers. To ensure that children and young people in care benefit from school based SRE and have any additional needs met, we will:

- **Set out in guidance how schools can support the SRE needs of young people in care.** This will include ensuring that children in care access the SRE offered by the school and that it is meeting their needs. Where the child or young person has additional needs, arrangements for one to one support or more intensive SRE should also be made in liaison with their social worker or foster carer.

5.28 Carers and social workers also have a vital role to play in ensuring that young people are able to make safe, confident and informed choices about sex and relationships. We set out in Chapter 3 the arrangements for including sexual health and relationship advice in residential and foster carer training. In addition we will:

- **Provide foster carers with tailored guidance on providing high quality sex and relationship education to the children and young people in their care.** The guidance will focus on helping children and young people develop the confidence to resist pressure to have early sex as well as providing the knowledge and skills to prevent unwanted pregnancy and to look after their sexual health when they do become sexually active; and

- **Ensure that social workers have the skills to assess whether SRE needs to be provided and understand how access can be provided to additional related support services.**

5.29 It is also vital that the specific needs of pregnant teenagers and teenage

The Healthy Schools programme is on track to achieve the Choosing Health commitment to have all schools gaining or working towards Healthy School status by 2009. As at May 2007 over 88% of schools were participating in the programme.

Evidence shows that children and young people in Healthy Schools feel healthier, happier and safer and the programme can bring sustained improvement in behaviour, standards of work and school management. This promotion of a more supportive environment, coupled with help to focus on the most vulnerable, makes the programme particularly relevant to meeting the needs of children in care.

parents in care or leaving care are fully met. In order to enable this, we will:

- **Ensure that they have a lead professional who co-ordinates a comprehensive package of support including:**

  - unbiased advice on pregnancy options and support in deciding what to do about their pregnancy;

  - if they choose to have the child, advocacy and support during the pregnancy, and after the child is born, with healthcare, benefits, educational opportunities and childcare;

  - access to a trusted adult who they can confide in, thereby enabling the early identification of difficulties and the provision of appropriate, co-ordinated support; and

  - advice on contraception to minimise the risk of subsequent unplanned pregnancies.

Play and positive activities

5.30 The impact of play on the health of children in care – and especially their mental health – is well established. Play is about fun and enjoyment. But imaginative play is also essential for children's development. It enables them to bring together their ideas, feelings, relationships and physical experiences. It allows them to use what they already know, so as to learn and understand more about the world they live in and the relationships around them.

5.31 Many children in care may not have had the same opportunity to play as other children, often resulting in serious negative effects on their social and emotional development.

5.32 Local authorities are currently being invited to work with local stakeholders to develop children's play strategies for their areas. The Big Lottery has allocated £124 million to local authorities to support this work and intends to fund projects that respond to the needs identified in these strategies.

5.33 The authority's strategy and associated funding provides an excellent opportunity to address the play requirements of children in care. The Big Lottery and Play England have already set out their expectation that authorities should focus on children in care as one of the groups with the poorest access to good play opportunities.

5.34 Safe and stimulating play also lies at the heart of the child's experience in Sure Start Children's Centres, where play based activities and facilities such as toy libraries are commonly available to carers.

5.35 More broadly the Government is promoting quality play through the *Birth to Three Matters* framework which provides examples of activities to promote play and learning, and through planned and spontaneous play activities within the Foundation Stage for three and four year olds. From September 2008 all settings offering early years provision will be required to deliver the

Fun and leisure

Healthy Care Partnerships in England have developed links with local and regional arts, sports, play and leisure providers to improve access to positive activities for children in care and their carers.

An example of this activity can be found in **Telford** where a Fun and Leisure Coordinator provides children in care with opportunities to experience a variety of arts and leisure projects. Fun and leisure plans are compiled as part of the care plan, and a range of activities provided.

Under this programme, some young people in care have made a successful application to the Youth Opportunity Fund to buy film-making equipment and studio time to create a film. They are also working in partnership with Telford and Wrekin Arts Team to create their own production company and take responsibility for all aspects of the film's production.

The young people are now set to gain their Arts Bronze Award and the film is being showcased in a 'first night premiere' organised by young people, as well as showing at the Telford and Wrekin Youth Arts Festival.

new Early Years Foundation Stage and from 2010 all 3 and 4 year-olds will be entitled to 15 hours per week of free early years provision for 38 weeks of the year. It is precisely because of the benefits offered by high-quality early years provision that we will ensure that social workers work with the carer and the local authority to arrange early years education for three and four year olds, as and when appropriate.

5.36 For older children and young people, involvement in organised leisure activities offers health and wellbeing benefits, providing opportunities to meet and interact with others and to develop friendships. This contact can counteract feelings of exclusion and provide valuable experiences in developing and maintaining social relationships. Evidence also suggests that exposure to trusted adults through these activities can help shape positive aspirations, beliefs and behaviours.

5.37 Involvement in structured positive leisure activities can also help young people make positive life choices and better transitions to adulthood and beyond. Self-esteem and an ability to rise to challenges and take up opportunities has a direct impact on educational attainment, success in the labour market, and avoiding negative outcomes such as teenage pregnancy and poor mental health including self-harm. Those with less well developed social and emotional skills can be left behind and be at risk of being socially excluded and developing anti-social behaviour.

National Standards for Positive Activities

- Access to two hours per week of sporting activity including formal and informal team and individual sports, outdoor and adventurous activities, and other physical activities such as aerobics and dance – provided through national curriculum and leisure-time activities.

- Access to two hours per week of other constructive activities in clubs, youth groups and classes. This includes activities in which young people pursue their interests and hobbies; activities contributing to their personal, social and spiritual development; activities encouraging creativity; innovation and enterprise; study support; and residential opportunities.

- Opportunities to make a positive contribution to their community through volunteering, including leading action, campaigning and fundraising.

- A wide range of other recreational, cultural, sporting and enriching experiences.

- A range of safe and enjoyable places in which to spend time. This could simply be somewhere to socialise with friends.

Transforming leisure time

5.38 Young people in care already have rights to leisure activities. The Education and Inspections Act 2006 placed a duty on local authorities to ensure that local young people have access to sufficient positive leisure time activities. The accompanying statutory guidance will make clear that the duty must be fulfilled with rigour in regard to children in care – taking account of their needs and ensuring that they are helped to overcome barriers to participation. The guidance will also specifically ask that authorities work towards providing the opportunities set out in national standards.

5.39 We know that the cost of activities is the primary reason why many children and young people do not participate in positive leisure time activities[5]. Meeting the national standards will therefore require that local authorities provide children and young people in care with free access to the positive activities and related facilities they own, deliver or commission. In doing so, authorities will be acting as responsible corporate parents, mirroring the support other children and young people receive from their parents in accessing after school and weekend activities.

5.40 Authorities will also need to listen to children and young people in care regarding the provision they value. The 2006 Act requires local authorities to consult and ensure that views are taken into account. For children in care, this might involve the use of questionnaires and focus groups, but central to the

---

5 *Care Matters* consultation responses. DfES (2007)

In order to ensure that children in care enjoy the same access to cultural life and the arts as their peers, the Museum, Library and Archives councils in the **North East of England and Yorkshire** introduced a "Max Card" scheme in 2004 whereby all children in care, their carers and carer's families can gain free access to a range of participating cultural attractions in their respective regions.

The scheme extends to over 90 museums and galleries in Yorkshire and the Humber, and 50 museums, galleries and heritage attractions across the North East.

In **Sefton** sport and leisure is viewed as an integral part of meeting the needs of a wide range of young people – in particular those who are disadvantaged or hard to reach. As part of the Council's Positive Futures programme two Leisure Inclusion Officers are jointly funded by the Council's Leisure Service and the emerging children's trust. The role of the officers, who form part of a multi-agency support team, is to ensure that children in care and those on the edge of care are able to access, and benefit from, sport and physical activity.

For children in care this includes:

- sport and leisure being included within placement plans;

- a 'leisure surgery' scheme where young people can be referred by their carers or other professionals for a one to one session with a development officer to explore their sport and leisure needs;

- provision of a free leisure pass entitling them to use of the Council's leisure facilities;

- access to a varied sports programme, including outdoor activities such as sailing; and

- access to an 'active lifestyle coach' who will work with them to develop personal programmes, improve their health and fitness and help them overcome any barriers to taking part in new or different activities.

consultation should be the Children in Care Council, whose opinions should help shape the local offer of activities[6].

5.41 Although local authorities offer a significant range of leisure time provision, many beneficial activities are also provided by schools, charities and businesses who may levy charges for participation. To address these cost barriers we will:

- **Provide significant new resources which, in combination with free local authority provision, will increase significantly the leisure opportunities for children in care.** This new funding reflects the Government's determination to

---

6 The HMT/DfES Aiming High for Disabled Children: Better Support for Families highlights the importance of increased availability of information and better transparency of individual entitlements, as key to empowering disabled individuals – allowing them to make more informed decisions and offering them the opportunity to be involved in the design and delivery of services.

ensure that children in care are first in line to benefit from enriching and enjoyable activities.

Removing cost barriers

5.42 We have already identified in Chapter 4 that children in care who are at risk of not reaching expected standards in education will be provided with a personalised annual budget of £500 to support their education. This funding will support participation in a wide range of positive activities linked to the personal education plan – both through paying fees for activities and also by providing the necessary equipment to engage in activities.

5.43 By having access to this funding in the form of an individual budget, children in care will be able to pay for provision without the risk of stigmatisation. The budget will also give children in care direct input into how the money is spent. It will be of particular benefit to disabled children in care who may face additional cost barriers.

5.44 In addition, we will also ask schools to ensure that children in care are eligible for free access to a varied menu of activities before and after school. Beginning with a large group of local authorities in 2009/10, and extended nationwide by 2010/11, we will:

- **Provide schools with funding to enable children in care to access 2 hours a week of extended school group activity, and two weeks of holiday provision free of charge.**

The virtual school head will have a key role in ensuring that schools respond to this opportunity both to support and to secure children's participation.

5.45 Furthermore, to ensure that children in care are not discouraged from participating in music tuition in schools during the school day, we will:

- **Introduce new regulations[7] to ensure that children in care will not be charged for music tuition in schools.**

5.46 We will also explore how we can better engage children in care in music-making. We will consult with them on the provision they already use and would like to use, as well as the factors that might limit their access to mainstream activity. We will look at existing music provision and explore best practice and the associated outcomes for children and young people. This exercise will provide us with an evidence base to share with schools and local authorities so that together we can consider how best to ensure that children in care access music provision.

5.47 Schools also play a key role in helping children and young people in care to access sporting activities. The National School Sport Strategy provides sporting opportunities for all school age children and young people, not only through the curriculum but also through school-to-club links and the Step into Sport volunteering programme. But we

---

7   Coming into force from September 2007

recognise that more can be done to ensure that community-based sport providers are able to engage effectively with those groups of children and young people – such as children in care – who are less likely to come forward and participate.

5.48 To provide this support, we will:

- **Work with the Youth Sport Trust and Sport England over the course of the 2007 Comprehensive Spending Review period to explore and support new approaches to providing community based sport opportunities for children in care.**

Youth activities

5.49 Young people in care will be significant beneficiaries of the Government's current review of youth services and support for young people. This review is due to report later in 2007 and will address the question of what strategy should be adopted over the next ten years to deliver a step change in youth services and support for young people.

5.50 In line with the Government's commitment to address disadvantage through ensuring that mainstream provision benefits vulnerable groups such as children in care, the ten year strategy and subsequent delivery arrangements will:

- **Ensure that young people at risk of poor outcomes, including children in care, significantly benefit from increased opportunities to take part in positive activities.**

Sky's Living For Sport initiative was launched in 2003 in partnership with the Youth Sport Trust. It offers a variety of sporting activities to develop leadership, team work and communication skills for 11-16 year olds in secondary schools across the UK. Olympic and world class sports champions act as mentors to the young people, making regular visits to the 500 participating schools across the UK.

70% of participating pupils demonstrate improvements in behaviour, social skills and self esteem, and 90% of these children maintain the improvements 12 months later.

In academic year 2005/06, **Sheffield's Educational Support Team** for children in care gave a group of young people who were in a mixture of foster, residential and family and friends care placements the opportunity to participate in the *Living For Sport* scheme and share its benefits. The young people were 14-16 years old. Late in the summer term, the programme was extended to Year 9 pupils (13-14 year olds) as a way of supporting their transition into Key Stage 4. Experiencing a number of sports activities through the process, the young people took on significant levels of responsibility and many developed supportive and mentoring skills.

According to one participant, *"I absolutely loved Sky's* Living For Sport, *it helped in loads of ways, like making me feel more confident."*

A dedicated youth worker

West Berkshire Council employs a youth worker for children in care. This person works with children and young people in care of all ages to help them access arts and other activities that are available through the Youth Service and through local arts initiatives.

The worker contacts young people by letter, through home visits, through foster carers' events and through respite sessions in the school holidays which she runs for 6-11 year old children.

Through this contact she finds out what young people are interested in and then signposts activities and supports attendance. The youth worker is part of the family placement team within children's services as well as the youth work team.

5.51 More broadly, the Government will ensure that the new performance management framework, as set out in the 2006 Government White Paper *Stronger and Prosperous Communities*, gives priority to increasing the number of young people on the path to success and provides a vehicle through which a range of Government departments will draw together their resource and planning to improve outcomes for children and young people.

5.52 Local authority youth work activities are central to the delivery of this objective, with a combined spend of over £400m a year on youth work activity. Youth work provision has not commonly focused on the needs of children in care, despite youth workers being ideally placed to support and encourage them. Working to a personal and social development curriculum and skilled in mentoring and counselling, youth workers are able to facilitate the development of young people in care in a range of informal settings.

5.53 The Government has already asked local authorities to adopt integrated approaches to meeting the needs of vulnerable groups and the support of youth workers for young people in care is entirely consistent with this approach. We will therefore:

- **Set out in guidance that the local authority must seek to improve outcomes for young people in care through involvement in youth work activity as a priority group – including through engagement with the Youth Opportunity Fund.**

5.54 To ensure that children in care can benefit from the 2012 Olympics and Paralympic Games we will also:

- **Establish a children in care sector reference group to guide DfES-sponsored Olympic activity; and**

- **Work with the 2012 Nations and Regions Group so that 2012 regional activities take account of children in care.**

5.55 We also know that many major companies already do valuable work with vulnerable children and young people in the community as part of their corporate social responsibility programmes, increasing their access to structured leisure activities and the world of work. While some of these opportunities are currently accessed by children and young people in care, we believe that more can be done, and that these children would benefit substantially from increased involvement with these programmes. We will therefore:

- **Work with a number of companies including HSBC, BT, BSkyB and Citi to further promote their involvement.**

Volunteering

5.56 Volunteering helps build skills and confidence. It provides new experiences and can raise aspirations and self esteem. For this reason it is included in the national standards for positive activities. Local authorities will therefore need to ensure that volunteering forms a central part of the offer of activities open to young people in care, including opportunities to volunteer within the authority itself.

5.57 Local authorities are also assisted by a range of voluntary bodies capable of providing children and young people in care with valuable voluntary experiences and placements. Central to this activity is the youth volunteering charity **v**, which was formed with the aim of involving at least 1 million more 16 – 25 year olds in volunteering and community action. The charity provides grants to voluntary sector bodies – through matching private with public funding – to ensure that dynamic and

valuable volunteering opportunities are available to young people.

5.58 To ensure children and young people in care are benefiting from this activity, we will:

- **Monitor the volunteering rates of children in care compared to their peers; and**

- **Should volunteering amongst children in care be shown to fall short of national averages, we will work with v to develop approaches by which we can boost their participation.**

Supporting participation

5.59 As with other important aspects of life for children in care, it is essential that engagement in positive activities is planned and supported. We will therefore:

- **Make clear in the revised care planning guidance that leisure activities should be included within the care plan of every child in care.** We will also indicate that care plans should address those factors that support participation, such as the provision of transport. This will be of particular relevance to disabled children in care and those living in rural areas.

5.60 For the planning process to work well, those involved in delivering the care plan will need to know what positive activities are available and how children in care can get involved. We will therefore:

- **Fund the production of packs for carers and children in care which will provide information on things to do and places to go in the local area.**

5.61 Based on a national template, the packs will be expected to build on, and make reference to, other information sources on positive activities – including young people's websites and other information developed through the £9m made available to local authorities between 2006-08 for this purpose.

5.62 By providing carers with packs, local authorities will also be helping to fulfil the requirements of section 12 of the Childcare Act 2006. This requires that local authorities provide information to carers of children on services that would benefit the child or young person – especially where the child or young person might otherwise miss out.

Beyond information

5.63 Although information about provision is essential, some children will need further support if they are to benefit from the opportunities available. Children and young people from all walks of life sometimes need encouragement to get involved in activities such as someone to help arrange their introduction, or accompany them to the activity.

5.64 For children in care this support can be vital in helping them overcome personal barriers to accessing opportunities relating to motivation,

aspirations and more serious problems. We will therefore:

- **Set out the expectation in statutory guidance that it is the role of the responsible social worker to ensure that children and young people in care receive appropriate support in accessing activities. This will be achieved through helping carers to:**

  - provide the children and young people in their care with activity packs and other information about play and positive activities – for example, through the authority's web-information on things to do and places to go, or by ensuring that the young person is registered to receive available text alerts on positive activity opportunities;

  - provide advice and encouragement, so children and young people can explore their options and the benefits of engagement;

  - ensure that the children and young people in their care get involved, e.g. by arranging for the provider to establish initial contact, by ensuring that the activity leader will make the child or young person welcome. To assist with this, the packs will provide key contact details of activity providers; and

  - provide support for the child to get involved by going with them and staying for the first few sessions and perhaps arranging for a friend of the child to join the activity too.

5.65 In recognition of the crucial role of the carer in supporting participation, we will also:

- **Ensure that foster carer training includes an understanding of the importance of play and leisure time activities, along with practical ways of supporting engagement.**

5.66 Supporting participation should not, however, be seen as the sole responsibility of the carer and social worker. Schools will need to ensure that children in care benefit from extended school activities and we will:

- **Set out in guidance our expectation that schools promote extended schools activities to children and young people in care and support their engagement.**

5.67 Independent Visitors are a further source of encouragement and support in accessing activities. Children and young people in care often view their Independent Visitor as a friend to talk to; someone who can provide them with emotional support and stability as well as enabling them to have fun and share in recreational activities. One study found that 'developing hobbies

Improving literacy

Knowsley Library Service's Right to Read Project aims to support the overall educational attainment of young people in care through promoting library use and the benefits of reading for pleasure.

The project works in partnership by:

- sharing in the delivery of a parent education programme, adapted to meet the needs of foster carers;

- engaging in preparation training for new carers and the professional development programme for established carers;

- offering creative arts workshops in the local library to young people from The KATY Project – a youth achievement programme for young people in care;

- supporting residential care workers in social services community homes through training, resources and enhanced library memberships;

- gifting books to children and young people directly and indirectly through other services for children in care e.g. through health assessment visits, social workers and education support workers; and

- developing the awareness of library staff and facilitating their links with Looked After Children's Services.

The project employs a part time co-ordinator and operates from Knowsley Library Service.

and interests' and 'increasing confidence' were the top two areas of support young care leavers thought a mentor could offer, ahead of support with work and training[8].

5.68 In recognition of the potential of the Independent Visitor to positively influence leisure time activity we will:

- **Ask local authorities to ensure Independent Visitors are both provided with activity packs to use with children and young people in care and understand the benefits of the activities they contain.**

Roles and responsibilities

5.69 For local partners to improve the health and wider wellbeing of children in care, they will need to show leadership and be clear about accountabilities and personal responsibilities.

5.70 *Promoting the health of looked after children*, DH (2002), already sets out some key individual roles with responsibility for representing the interests of children in care within relevant organisations. These roles include the designated doctor and nurse who provide clinical and strategic oversight on issues affecting children in care.

5.71 We also believe that children in care should have a strong focus at PCT board level. *Promoting the Health of Looked After Children* already asks PCT

Chief Executives to ensure that the health and wellbeing of children and young people in care are an identified local priority. We will therefore:

- **Ensure that this role is identified in statutory guidance and thereby secure a strong PCT board level focus on children in care.**

To support the Chief Executive in fulfilling this role we will:

- **Explore how the portfolio of the senior lead for children and young people in PCTs[9] can be developed to address further the needs of vulnerable groups of children – including children in care.**

Local authority responsibilities

5.72 In keeping with the role of corporate parent, the Director of Children Services (DCS) will also need to ensure that the health and wellbeing of children in care are addressed. We will:

- **Set out in statutory guidance that the DCS should utilise the JSNA and the Children and Young People's Plan for this purpose, and ensure that the Director of Public Health is contributing to the understanding of children in care's health needs within the children's trust.**

5.73 The DCS will also need to ensure that local joint commissioning arrangements are able to secure adequate CAMHS for children in care.

---

8   The Princes Trust (April 2002) *The way it is.*

9   See Department of Health (2004) National Service Framework for Children, Young People and Maternity Services

5.74 To ensure that the investment in children and young people's leisure time is well utilised we will:

- **Make clear in statutory guidance that it is the responsibility of the Director of Children's Services (DCS) to ensure that children in care are enjoying similar or better levels of engagement in positive activities as other children and young people of their age. The Lead Member will also have a role in ensuring that the DCS is fulfilling this responsibility.**

5.75 In order to measure progress on the participation of children in care, we will encourage DCSs to gather information in a number of ways, including:

- through the data provided by the local authorities' Integrated Youth Support Service (IYSS);

- reviewing the progress of individual children in care through the care planning process; and

- asking the virtual head to provide feedback on the extent of participation in extended school activities by children in care.

5.76 More broadly, the local authority and healthcare bodies will wish to draw upon the scrutiny, information and assessment provided through the new Joint Area Review arrangements which include from 2007 a more in-depth focus on children in care. The new JAR arrangements will not only provide useful feedback on performance in regard to the access of children in care

to positive activities, but will clearly address the role of health services assessing and meeting their needs.

5.77 Specific elements inspectors may consider include whether the health needs of children in care are assessed at a sufficiently early stage to enable effective interventions and the impact of foster carer and residential staff training in understanding and meeting these needs. Inspectors may also consider whether jointly commissioned and delivered services including pooled budgets are having a discernible impact in improving outcomes for children in care.

5.78 In addition to the DCS, local authority members will also have an important role to play in addressing the health needs of children in care. Subject to the will of Parliament, provisions in the Local Government and Public Involvement in Health Bill will provide local authority elected members with strengthened powers to require PCTs, NHS trusts and NHS Foundation Trusts to co-operate with overview and scrutiny committees in the provision of information. These same bodies will also be under a duty to have regard to recommendations of the committees when exercising their functions.

5.79 Through these new powers we will

- **Provide local authorities with important new opportunities to improve co-ordination and challenge healthcare bodies' contribution to the wellbeing of children in care.**

Chapter 6
Transition to adulthood

"I would like to have a trial to see if I can handle moving out, or I want it. That way I have the choice to go back home if I can't cope."

Young person

Summary

Many children receive excellent support from carers and leaving care services but too often young people in care move into adult life without being prepared or supported: 27% of "care leavers" (those who were in care aged sixteen or over) still leave care at 16: a time when most of their peers are concentrating on education, not fending for themselves. Reasonable parents would not want their children to be left on their own and unsupported at that age. Any good parent will continue to offer love and support to their children well beyond 18, giving them the greatest head start in life that they can. The Government expects no less for young people in care, and this chapter sets out our plans to:

- Pilot greater involvement of young people in deciding when they move to independence;

- Provide young people with the opportunity to benefit from staying with foster carers – or, if appropriate, in residential care – until age 21;

- Provide personal adviser support for those who haven't achieved the qualifications they need by the age of 21, and to those young adults who request additional support up to 25;

- Place £100 per year in the Child Trust Fund account of every eligible child who spends the year in care; and

- Introduce a national bursary, requiring local authorities to provide a minimum of £2,000 for all young people in care who go on to University.

Introduction

6.1 Transition to adulthood is often a turbulent time for young people, and over the last generation becoming an adult has changed significantly. Transitions are no longer always sequential – leave school, work, marriage, setting up home, parenthood. Young people can become adult in one area but not in others.

6.2 For many young adults in today's world, the transition to adulthood can be extended and delayed until they are emotionally and financially ready, and have obtained the right qualifications to offer them the opportunity to achieve their economic potential. But adolescence continues to be a period of experimentation and young people face greater risks than the rest of the population, particularly in relation to homelessness, unemployment, and crime. Most young people know they can call on the support of their families to help them through unforeseen difficulties.

6.3 For young people in care the move to adulthood is often more difficult. The opportunity to delay adulthood until they are financially and emotionally ready is not always open to them, leading to an accelerated transition. Evidence indicates that young people without parental and family support are exposed to greater risks than other adolescents.

6.4 In addition, there is an expectation that young people leaving the care system will have the skills necessary to cope on their own such as managing limited finances, cooking, cleaning, and paying the rent. Coupled with potentially transient placements, this can be an unstable platform for adulthood.

6.5 The Government's ambition is to help young people prepare for adulthood, and facilitate young people leaving care at the most appropriate time for them so that they are properly prepared, and feel ready to make a successful transition to adulthood.

Extract from *Outcome Indicators for Looked After Children: Twelve Months to 30 September 2006*, England. DfES April 2007

- At the end of school year 11, 64% of children in care remained in full-time education compared to 78% of all school-leavers.

- 20% were unemployed the September after leaving school compared to 5% of all school-leavers.

- In 2005, 61% of children in care remained in full-time education compared to 75% for all school-leavers.

- 9.6% of children in care aged 10 or over were cautioned or convicted for an offence during the year, almost 3 times the rate for all children of this age. This rate has been similar over the past 3 years.

A more personalised and stable approach

6.6 We recognise that transition to adulthood is particularly challenging for disabled young people. The Government has announced through *Aiming High for Disabled Children: Better Support for Families* the Transition Support programme, a model based on the principles of the early years programme to help improve transition planning and services to better enable and support disabled young people in their transition to adult life.

6.7 Young people in care should expect the same level of care and support from their carers that others would expect from a reasonable parent. The local authority responsible for their care should be making sure that they are provided with this. We should not expect young people to make changes that would be difficult for any 16 year old – let alone for vulnerable 16 year olds – where the local authority has had to assume responsibility for their care.

6.8 No local authority should be able to make a significant change, such as a move from a care placement to so called 'independent' accommodation, without both the proposal being rigorously scrutinised under the established care planning process and the child confirming that they understand the implications of any proposed change and positively agree to it.

Right2B Cared4

6.9 Responses to the recent consultation indicated overwhelming support for young people aged 16-18 years to be given a voice in the decision making process that can change placement

---

Transition Support Programme

The Government has announced a £19m Transition Support Programme, over 2008-11, to improve the transition into adulthood for disabled young people. The Programme will include:

- a young person's information pack;

- access to an advisor or key worker;

- choice and control for young people, including support in making decisions about their future;

- planning centred around the needs of the young person; and

- joint team working across agencies and with adult services.

The Programme will cover the particular needs of disabled children in care, including clarifying who has lead responsibility for those placed out-of-authority, supporting independence and offering the same range of opportunities that other young people take for granted.

arrangements, whether that be residential or foster care. The Government supports this view, and we will:

- **Pilot, from September 2007, the involvement of young people in the decision making process that influences their care – Right2B Cared4.**

6.10 The pilots are currently being tendered for, and we intend to legislate and move to national coverage by 2010.

6.11 Under this pilot, significant changes to a young person's care plan – such as a change to move to an independent placement[1] – will only be permissible where these follow as a result of a properly constituted statutory review of the child's care plan chaired by an Independent Reviewing Officer (IRO).

6.12 All information relevant to the child's future must be made available to a review meeting. This must include a thorough up-to-date assessment of the child's needs so that the evidence supporting any proposal to change the young person's placement is clear and well understood. Where such evidence is unavailable then the IRO would require the authority to postpone the review and therefore any proposal to change the young person's plan.

6.13 The assessment of the young person's needs must take full account of the young person's wishes and feelings and their active participation must be at the heart of the review.

6.14 All young people being faced with the possibility of having to move to "independence" should be supported by an independent person (nominated by the young person) throughout the review process to ensure that they are given the opportunity to express their wishes and feelings and that they fully understand the implications of any proposal.

6.15 Where, exceptionally, the outcome of the review leads to actions that set aside the wishes and feelings of the young person concerned the authority must follow its dispute resolution process.

6.16 No changes will impact on a young person while the dispute resolution process is ongoing.

6.17 We have listened to views of stakeholders regarding the increase of access to advocates for young people in care. The Right2B Cared4 pilots will enable us to test whether young people have particular preferences in choosing independent advocates and how far access to advocacy contributes to improved outcomes and the quality of young people's engagement in planning their care.

Placements post 18

6.18 The average age young people leave home is 24 years. Yet if a young person is in foster care they will usually leave their placement at 18 years. Young people in foster care can develop

---

1 An "independent" placement will be defined as one that is not regulated under the Care Standards Act 2000

strong relationships and emotional attachments with those who care for them, and young people told us that they wanted to have the option to stay with foster carers where such relationships and attachments have developed.

6.19 We will:

- **Pilot arrangements, from 2008-09, for young people who have established familial relationships with their foster carers to continue to stay with them up to the age of 21.**

6.20 Alongside this, the Government is committed to changing the way that foster carers are assessed for claiming benefits when they continue to care for a young person beyond their 18th birthday. These young people are legally adults, so can no longer be regarded as a "child in foster care" for benefit purposes.

6.21 At present payments to ex-carers in these circumstances are taken into account in assessing their benefit entitlements, creating a disincentive to offer continuity of care to care leavers. **In order that payments to former foster carers are disregarded and treated in the same way as the fostering allowance they will have received before the young person's 18th birthday, we will:**

- **Make the necessary regulatory change by Spring 2008.**

Young people leaving children's homes

6.22 Young people placed in children's homes can be a particularly vulnerable group. Local authorities too often treat a placement in a children's home as a "last resort" yet a children's home placement could well be the right setting for meeting young people's

Support for care leavers

Hull established the Young People's Support Service (YPSS) in response to a report that highlighted the accommodation difficulties faced by young people moving on from care, and other young people facing crises. The aim of the YPSS is to provide a 'one stop shop' multidisciplinary service, including a Supported Lodgings Service.

The Supported Lodgings Service provides practical and financial support to all care leavers who need it. Working closely with co-located fostering services, the service facilitates the continuation of foster placements for those over 18 (or sooner if an order is discharged) until they are 21. These continued placements are viewed as supported lodgings and as such receive a weekly allowance that has been explicitly set to match the mainstream fostering allowance for the young adults involved. There is no disincentive for carers to continue to provide a placement for young people.

Of the 46 supported lodgings for care leavers 17 have transferred from fostering placements, freeing up other supported lodgings. 97% of these young people are in education, employment or training.

needs and supporting them to prepare for the transition to adult life.

6.23 Where young people depend on children's homes for their care, it is important that they are provided with the necessary stability needed to move into adult life. Providing quality care while completing education will give young people the opportunity they need to reach their potential.

6.24 We want to ensure that there is detailed scrutiny of any proposal in a care plan that recommends moving a young person from a placement regulated under the Care Standards Act 2000 (like a children's home or foster care) to any unregulated placement (such as a hostel or "independence" flat). We will be legislating to ensure that young people are not moved from regulated to unregulated placements unless such a proposal has been properly scrutinised. The review process will give due weight to the young person's own views. Any recommendation will need to ensure that the young person has been properly prepared to manage any move and that the planned move will meet all the young person's needs – for example continuity of education.

6.25 This will support the placement stability of those young people who rely on the children's home sector for their care – particularly important for those young people who are in year 13 and have not completed their schooling.

6.26 By the time young people reach legal adulthood at 18, most should have been properly prepared for the next step in making their transition to adulthood. For example, this might involve a move to supported lodgings or other form of accommodation perhaps linked to the children's home where they may have lived for a number of years.

6.27 The Right2B Cared4 pilots will be especially relevant for children in children's homes as we know that this group of young people are likely to be those who often feel "forced" to leave their care placement at 16 and move to a so called "independence" placement, with little real support to make sure that they can cope emotionally and practically with living on their own. These pilots are designed to ensure that young people are only expected to leave their care placement after full consultation and preparation so that "moving-on" is a welcome progression which occurs when the young person feels ready after they have completed their secondary education.

6.28 Where young people have been placed in residential care, it is less likely that they will have established a 'family' attachment with the adults caring for them. However, during the course of the 'staying with foster carers until 21' pilots we will look to see if there is demand by young people to stay in children's homes beyond 18. We will then consider what approaches could work in those circumstances.

Gaining skills to live independently

6.29 Before a young person can move to independent living it will be important that the plan for their continuing support (their "pathway plan") is based on a thorough, comprehensive, assessment of their needs, taking their wishes and feelings into account. This will include assessing whether the young person has all the skills that they will need to manage in any future accommodation. This assessment should then influence how young people will be matched to any prospective "independent" accommodation.

6.30 Based on the issues identified as part of the assessment process, carers and other agencies (e.g. Connexions or, for a young parent, parenting support services) will have a key role in equipping care leavers with the right skills to enable them to make a positive transition to moving on from their placement.

6.31 Young people living with their families are often given the opportunities to learn the skills required for independent living. Living in a family environment gives young people scope to acquire an understanding of cooking, cleaning and other skills required for successful independent living. Even simple things like knowing how to use a washing machine or that rubbish bins are only collected on certain days are important.

6.32 However, those young people who live in residential care homes and some

---

A chance to help others

Lewisham care leavers were involved in a volunteering project, South East London to South Africa (SELSA). Run in conjunction with the sister authority Ekurhuleni, near Johannesburg, it was the first of its kind in the UK.

11 young people moving on from care participated and secured funding for the project through a variety of fundraising initiatives and by submitting applications for grants, all while securing education, employment and training opportunities for themselves.

The volunteers travelled to South Africa and mixed with young people from similar backgrounds, visiting and helping out on community projects. The young people also spent time at a wildlife rehabilitation centre, where they learnt practical veterinary and outdoor skills and developed teamwork and interpersonal skills.

The volunteers demonstrated motivation and determination throughout the project, showing how young people in care can make an immense, valued and positive contribution to their communities. The experience was an intense one for the group, and tested the young people by taking them away from the familiar and showing them what is possible with hard work and commitment. It has had a profound effect on the lives of the young people both on an emotional level, but also as a catalyst for positive lifestyle changes. Indeed many of the volunteers want to become peer mentors for other children in care.

foster homes do not always have experience of these things and miss out on the opportunities to learn these skills. Any parent would want to address this.

6.33 As detailed in Chapter 3, as part of package of improved training provision for carers, we will provide training so that carers can acquire the skills needed to help young people, including those with complex needs and disabilities, learn the practicalities of living alone.

Continuing support

6.34 Most people recognise that you do not stop being a parent when children leave home. Those young people who live with their families will continue to benefit from emotional and often financial support, sometimes well into their twenties. Yet young people in care are expected to survive on their own resources with limited support.

6.35 The Government wants to encourage an approach which continues to support care leavers as long as they need it, which ceases to talk about 'leaving care' and instead ensures that young people move on in a gradual, phased and, above all, prepared way. This should mean that young people are provided with the necessary support at the right time, for example support in finding moving on accommodation after the 'straight from care' placement if needed. As a result care leavers can make a smoother transition to adulthood which is more in line with the way that other young people leave home.

6.36 As we move towards the proposed changes to post 16 education[2], it is vital

The right support at the right time

Barry had a history of threatening behaviour leading to placement breakdowns. When he reached 18, Barry decided he wanted to go into the army, but it became clear he needed support to pursue an application.

A member of the aftercare team in Wiltshire County Council, who had previously had a career in the army, used the team's working relationship with the local Army Careers Office to discuss Barry, and to raise his concerns that Barry would not pass his physical assessment.

Barry was accompanied at all his recruitment appointments by an army recruitment officer. The army also allowed him to run a dummy physical assessment—something it rarely does. The aftercare worker supported Barry through gym sessions so he could improve his fitness.

As a result of all this support Barry was successful in joining the army, and the aftercare worker recently attended his passing out parade from basic training.

Wiltshire is now building on this partnership: the army recruitment service has agreed to lead sessions on career opportunities at a residential week for 10 young people leaving care

2   Raising Expectations: staying in education and training post-16 DfES March 2007

that young people in care receive support from their corporate parents when they are considering the education and training options open to them. The Government expects local authorities to ensure that personal advisers, social workers, and foster carers have access to information regarding schools, targeted youth support services and other services that can signpost young people in their care towards appropriate information, advice and guidance to help young people make the best choices for them.

6.37 Not only is information regarding education and training important, but young people in care need also to be offered other opportunities that help them make a successful transition to adulthood. These opportunities can include voluntary work – allowing young people to experience different aspects of the community in which they live. To support this we will:

- **Disseminate evidence about the outcomes of models of volunteering-based work for young people in care.**

6.38 Moving into employment for any young person can be daunting. But for some young people this is eased by their parents, who will use contacts and scan job adverts to help their children into work. Corporate parents should do the same. Local authorities, their partners and all public sector employers have huge potential to offer work with

Apprenticeships

Lincolnshire and their partners, Connexions and Barnardo's (including a training provider –HBS Options) have developed the **Care Leavers Apprenticeship Scheme** (CLAS).

The scheme provides care leavers with access to a modern apprenticeship within the county council's directorates, local district councils and other employers. The Executive Councillors support the scheme. Nominated officers within each directorate champion the apprenticeship scheme, and identify potential placements. It is intended that up to 20 care leavers will be placed with the county council alone.

CLAS aims to broaden the range of opportunities for young people, to offer a more comprehensive range of apprenticeships and to develop new opportunities. Care leavers will enter the programme with different levels of needs as they make the transition into employment. The scheme will address these needs, ranging from basic literacy and numeracy skills and personal presentation to the more complex issues such as personal management, addictions and homelessness.

During their participation in the apprenticeship scheme, they gain a strong foundation in key skills. As their confidence and experience improves, they are encouraged to apply for suitable vacancies within the County Council.

training or apprenticeships to young people who have been in care.

6.39 As corporate parents, the whole public sector has a responsibility to examine the work experience and employment with training opportunities they can make available to children in care. Once identified these opportunities should be highlighted in the children in care pledge outlined in Chapter 1. Local authorities will also want to champion young people leaving care so that they do not experience discrimination when looking for work.

6.40 As well as apprenticeships we need to explore other employment and training opportunities for young people in care. Many young people moving on from care may need more support and encouragement than their peers if they are to enter management training programmes. Both private and public sector employers need to facilitate opening up these programmes to young people who have been in care.

Unaccompanied asylum seeking children (UASC)

6.41 Unaccompanied asylum seeking children (UASC) are in this country without any adult to care for them and it is appropriate for most of these young people to enter local authority care. They will be entitled to the same range of support as all other children in care. They must have a care plan based on a thorough assessment of their needs and this plan will be subject to regular reviews chaired by Independent Reviewing Officers. Over the age of 16, UASC care leavers will be entitled to services and support as they prepare to move on from care; their care plan will become the "pathway plan" and they should be allocated a personal adviser.

6.42 Unlike other care leavers, UASC will have an immigration status and an outstanding asylum claim. Pathway planning for these young people is concerned with providing them with the skills and services necessary so that they can make a successful transition to adulthood in their home communities. For the small minority whose asylum claim is accepted, their community will

Opening up management training programmes

HSBC has this year launched its Management Academy Programme (MAP). The programme is for over 18s who are looking for training and skills development. It provides a springboard for young people, with paid on-the-job training and a clear career in sight.

Building on this, HSBC will make additional resources available to pilot a programme which provides a bridge for care leavers into the Management Academy Programme.

The "Access to MAP" programme is intended to give care leavers the opportunity to work for HSBC and attend college on a day release basis where they will work towards appropriate vocational qualifications.

be the UK. However, 95% of asylum claims are refused and young people will need to be prepared to be resettled in their countries of origin. Therefore, the pathway planning process must also be relevant to the circumstances and needs of those UASC who will be required to return to their countries of origin.

6.43 The Home Office issued a consultation paper in March 2007 setting out proposals for improving the quality and timeliness of asylum decision making for UASC. These proposals would provide the opportunity for a more personalised approach to planning for UASC to better co-ordinate casework on asylum applications with the pathway planning process.

Access to a personal adviser to 25

6.44 Personal advisers have a critical role to play in helping young people make decisions that are best for them and ensuring that timely support is available. Young people who have experienced care currently have access to a personal adviser until the age of 21. However, young people have told us that they would welcome access to this support beyond age 21. We will therefore:

- **Extend the provision of a personal adviser (PA) and maintain a pathway plan to:**

  - Every care leaver who by the age of 21 has still to achieve the educational qualifications or training they feel are necessary for their future; and

  - Any young person up to the age of 25, previously a care leaver, who asks for assistance with further learning or training – including, of course, any care leaver aged 21+ who having achieved a basic qualification wishes then to take up their entitlement to qualifications at higher levels.

6.45 We are aware that some disabled young people may progress at a slower rate than their peers because of the additional complexity of their needs and for these young people, access to a PA post 21 will be an important benefit. However for those young people whose disability results in needs sufficient to warrant access to adult community care services we do not anticipate replacing that support with PA support.

Further education

6.46 Some young people in care face disruption to their initial education and miss substantial parts of their schooling. The reforms set out in Chapters 3 and 4 aim to tackle that disruption.

6.47 But we need to ensure that young people are given the opportunity to take advantage of learning at later stages. To do that they need the right advice and assistance to take advantage of a range opportunities, including Further Education (FE).

6.48 The entitlement to a personal advisor until the age of 25 will give young people the maximum opportunity to take advantage of their entitlement to free first time level 2 and Level 3 learning. But it is essential that the FE system is flexible enough to support young people in re-engaging with their learning. To help meet this need we will:

- **Explore the possibility of flexible starting dates for young people who want to pursue Diplomas and other qualifications in an FE setting; and**

- **Introduce progression pathways within the Foundation Learning Tier that enable young people to progress to level 2 learning.** This will include a new pre-Apprenticeship pathway that will provide young people with a work-based learning route.

6.49 We will also target young people in care and their carers in recruitment programmes for literacy, language and numeracy skills courses and the development of a Family Literacy and Language Learning package for those in care and their carers.

6.50 The transition of young people in care from school to FE is not always supported by a good exchange of information. It is not always easy for FE providers to identify the extra support many young people in care will need. This is a gap that needs filling. As previously set out we will:

- **Improve the sharing of data on children in care, via the Managing Information Across Partners project, so that we can track participation, progression and**

attainment of children in care as they move from school to college and other learning; and

- **Develop a self-assessment tool kit for FE institutions to evaluate the effectiveness of the support they are offering to children in care.**

6.51 Additionally one of the tests and trials being undertaken for the Managing Information Across Partners work in the Manchester 14-19 Partnership area is also looking at how a Learner Registration Service and unique learner number can help local organisations provide better support to children in care. Those tests and trials are currently underway and will be reporting later in the year.

6.52 Colleges and the FE sector have an excellent record in supporting young people with a commitment to learning but who need extra support to achieve their potential. We want to ensure that the particular needs of young people in care are understood and prioritised across the FE sector, and are committed to:

- Including training on the needs of children in care as part of the new Principals' Qualifying Programme, which will be mandatory for new principals;

- Including a module within the professionalisation programme for Skills for Life professionals which will help them meet the needs of children in care; and

- Developing a pilot on pastoral support to help FE providers better meet the personal needs of children in care and care leavers.

Accommodation

6.53 Not all young people will want to or are able to stay in their placements beyond 18. Additionally they may lack the usual support networks provided by parents and friends and therefore have a particular need for support. For these young people supported accommodation provides a valuable option.

6.54 At all the consultations we had with young people, accommodation has been raised as a very pressing and real issue for them. Young people have told us they want more choice in accommodation and some would welcome the opportunity to try out living independently before they take the plunge. We support this view, and know that some local authorities are giving young people the opportunity to understand what it would be like coping on their own.

6.55 We are committed to increasing the range of supported accommodation available. But future development of supported accommodation for care leavers must be based on high quality evidence about effective models of service delivery supported by strong partnership working between housing agencies and services for children in and leaving care.

6.56 We are commissioning work to identify models of best practice in delivering housing support services to vulnerable young people, and we remain committed to developing a capital investment fund, with the Housing Corporation, to support the provision of dedicated accommodation for young people and to increase their accommodation choices.

6.57 We know young people who leave care are concerned about homelessness. Good practice authorities have established move on arrangements for care leavers through a range of approaches such as quotas from supported housing in the private rented sector and choice based lettings schemes for social housing. These 'pathways' ensure young care leavers have planned routes to settled housing. Floating support and resettlement services, commissioned jointly, are effective in reducing the likelihood of young people losing their accommodation.

6.58 Ongoing support through the implementation of a young person's pathway plan should avoid homelessness. However, where such arrangements break down, the homelessness legislation provides an essential safety net, where necessary.

6.59 The Government's strategy for tackling homelessness, *Sustainable Communities: settled homes; changing lives*, recognises that young people can become homeless for a wide range of often complex reasons. 16 and 17 year olds

A taste of independence

Solihull have secured a rented 2 bedroom flat for the sole use of young people in their care.

The flat allows young people to get a taste of independent living before embarking on it permanently and the young people can stay for anything from one weekend to 4 weeks. The flat is managed by the 16+ team and while young people are at the flat they are supported to develop life skills including budgeting, shopping, cooking and self care skills. Support workers will continue to work with the young people once they have left the flat and until they are settled in accommodation, be that independent living or supported accommodation.

This approach has enabled young people to assess for themselves what it means to live independently, what challenges they will face and how to cope. In 2006-07 13 young people used the flat and the majority have moved successfully to independent living.

and young people aged between 18 and 20 who were formerly in care have priority need for accommodation under the homelessness legislation. This means they must be secured suitable accommodation if they become homeless through no fault of their own. In these cases, children's services are expected to provide suitable support services to enable the young care leaver to sustain their accommodation.

6.60 **We are commissioning good practice guidance on housing and children's services co-operation regarding homelessness. This will include guidance on working together to meet the specific needs of young people leaving care.** We will continue to work with and consult with non statutory organisations to develop this guidance.

6.61 We will continue to work with Rainer on *What Makes the Difference*, and the *National Leaving Care Advisory Service*

to make further improvements to accommodation services for care leavers.

Health Services

6.62 Those leaving care, like all young adults, need to be able to access appropriate health services.

6.63 There is a risk that adolescents can fall between children's and adult's health services, with neither meeting young people's needs: confidentiality; privacy and communication skills; and knowledge of the basic biological and psychological changes of adolescence.

6.64 Up to now, very few targeted services exist in England, and teenagers report concerns and difficulties about using their GP service: citing difficulty in getting an early appointment, embarrassment, and doubt about confidentially and unsympathetic doctors. This is a key issue for all young people, but especially vulnerable care leavers.

6.65 In response to these challenges *'You're Welcome'* quality criteria have been established, setting out minimum standards for all health care settings to ensure they are young people friendly. One of the minimum standards is that PCTs should have in place local strategies to promote easier access to services by marginalised groups including children in care and care leavers.

6.66 Four Teenage Health Demonstration Sites in Bolton, Hackney, Northumberland and Portsmouth were launched in August 2006. The sites will explore and evaluate how services can become better equipped and coordinated to meet the health needs of young people aged 11-19 – particularly the 30% most vulnerable. The sites will showcase the application of *'You're Welcome'*. The Department of Health will work with the Sites, Government Offices and other partners, to develop a 'Quality Mark' to identify designated *'You're Welcome'* health services.

6.67 The demonstration site programme is being systematically evaluated and the learning will be fed into future commissioning frameworks and inspection systems so that it becomes embedded into mainstream activity. The Department of Health is also working with the Royal College of Paediatrics and Child Health to develop a training scheme in adolescent medicine for all doctors working with teenagers.

Financial support

6.68 Financial support for young people in care to enter adult life is highly variable between local authorities and relies on subjective judgements as to the level of support required. Young people have told us that they think this is particularly unfair.

6.69 Research[3] has found that the most common weekly allowance paid across 52 leaving care teams was £42.70 and that the grant paid to young people on leaving care varied from £400 in some local authorities to as much as £2,000 in others. The local authority is left to make a judgement as to the level of support required and young people do not always feel they get what they need.

6.70 We have listened to these concerns and confirm our commitment that we will:

- **Invest £100 per year in the Child Trust Fund account of every child who spends the year in care, starting in 2008.**

Going on to higher education

6.71 The Government has set out its ambition to increase participation in higher education towards 50 per cent of those aged 18 to 30 by 2010. Alongside this, the Government wants to widen participation so that more people from backgrounds that currently under represented have the opportunity to participate in higher education. This includes young people in care.

---

3   National Leaving Care Advisory Service Benchmarking Forum Survey, 2005

Collaborative working

Leeds social services and education agencies work collaboratively to assist young people in care to reach their higher education ambitions.

Noreen lived at home with her mother and 6 siblings. Her mother had little command of English and felt overwhelmed by British society. Noreen became the main carer and advocate for her family, a situation which led to her struggling.

Noreen's mother was given the support she needed to cope with the family. This reduced and limited the responsibility placed on Noreen, giving her more time to focus on her educational studies.

Noreen, as well as having access to personal and financial assistance, was given a laptop. This allowed Noreen to achieve her ambition to enter higher education. Noreen is now at university and has no doubt that this wouldn't have been possible without the joint collaboration of social services and education agencies.

6.72 The commitments we have given in Chapter 4 to improve attainment of young people in care at school are part of that ambition, but we do recognise that young people from care face some barriers to entering higher education. In order to address these barriers:

- **The University and College Admissions Service (UCAS) will introduce a tick box on their applications, from September 2008**, so that applicants coming from care backgrounds can be identified and supported during the admission process and once they begin their studies.

6.73 The response to the consultation showed overwhelming support for our proposal to tackle the financial constraints which students from care backgrounds face compared to their peers. As previously stated, from April 2008 we are committed to:

- **Introducing a national bursary, requiring local authorities to provide a minimum of £2,000 for all young people in care who go onto University.**

6.74 Improving support to young people while they are studying is equally important and the other recommendations set out in the *Care Matters* Green Paper were supported. We remain committed to giving young people a choice of vacation accommodation while they are studying.

6.75 A task group was established to look at how Aimhigher and other higher education outreach activity can be better targeted on young people from lower socio-economic groups, including children in care. The Higher Education Funding Council for England (HEFCE) published good practice guidance *'Higher education: targeting disadvantaged learners'* in May 2007.

Improving access to higher education

The **Frank Buttle Trust** commissioned research on the challenges faced by young people moving from care to university. This work resulted in the Quality Mark, which sets out the specific requirements that higher education providers need to meet in order to improve the access, experiences and support of care leavers entering higher education.

Interest is growing as universities are becoming increasingly aware of the need to support students who are care leavers to achieve their full potential. **Loughborough University Development Trust** has successfully appealed to former students, staff and supporters of the University to fund a three-year full-time PhD Research Studentship, based at its Centre for Child and Family Research.

The purpose of the study will be to explore whether, and in what ways, the experience of care leavers in higher education has changed since the introduction of new policies intended to widen participation in higher education and initiatives specifically aimed at improving outcomes for looked after children. The very generous response to the appeal will also fund bursaries for care leavers coming to Loughborough University.

This is an excellent example of how different organisations and communities can work together to ensure that care leavers, along with all other young people, have better opportunities to reach their full potential.

6.76 In December 2006, the Office for Fair Access (OFFA) made a statement asking higher education institutions (HEIs) to consider how access agreements address the needs of young people who have been in care. OFFA has also highlighted the Frank Buttle Trust Quality Mark. This Quality Mark, launched in June 2006, has now been awarded to 11 universities, with a further 19 applications under consideration.

6.77 In addition, OFFA has ensured that its website prominently displays a link to the DfES's online bursary map. This and the DirectGov Student Finance website, can also be accessed from the students' page of the OFFA website.

6.78 We remain committed to encouraging HEIs and colleges to offer support for children in care through mentoring and the development and dissemination of training packages for staff in HEIs, and to have in place a member of staff with expertise and responsibility for supporting care leavers.

Chapter 7
The role of the practitioner

"We got on really well. I spoke to her about my problems and she treated me as a grown up as she knew my history and knew that with my Mum dying I had to grow up really quickly. She also knew I could work things out for myself and when I had arguments with my foster carers she didn't really have to get involved because I would eventually work them out."

Young person[1]

Summary

In practice, the Corporate Parent is embodied for children in care by the professionals they see on a day to day basis. This chapter sets out how we will ensure that the child experiences a seamless service which is consistent, responsive to need, and receptive to their wishes and feelings. Our approach comprises:

- **Workforce remodelling, to enable social workers to spend more time with the child;**

- **Reforms to the training of social workers to ensure that they are knowledgeable in the relevant theoretical frameworks such as child development and attachment and well prepared in practice for the new children's services arrangements;**

- **Developing tailored recruitment campaigns to emphasise the particular benefits of working in a children's services environment;**

- **Introducing a "Newly Qualified Social Worker" status that would give a guarantee of support, training and induction to child and family social workers;**

- **Piloting 'Social Work Practices' in order to test whether partnership with external agencies can improve the child's experience of care, and empower the local authority to exercise their corporate parenting function more effectively;**

- **Reforms to the independent reviewing system to ensure that Independent Reviewing Officers (IROs) provide more effective monitoring of care planning on behalf of the child; and**

- **Ensuring that all those children in care who need them have access to independent visitors and to independent advocates.**

---

1   Skuse, T. and Ward, H. (forthcoming) Children's Views of Care and and Accommodation, London: Jessica Kingsley Publishers

Introduction

7.1 Our reforms to services for children in care depend on having a highly skilled, valued, committed and stable workforce that delivers individualised support to children and young people. Local areas are reforming the children's workforce to work in new ways, through multi-agency teams, with better information sharing and common processes such as the Common Assessment Framework (CAF)[2] and ContactPoint[3]. Reform of the school workforce is enabling better, more personalised learning by freeing up the teacher to support the needs of individual pupils.

7.2 Respondents to the *Care Matters* consultation felt strongly that reform of the social care workforce in direct contact with children and young people was important and that capacity and quality needed to be increased. We know that there are many highly skilled and able managers and practitioners who work with children in care and make a big difference to their lives. However, children and young people wanted more stability and for social workers to listen and have more time for them. More needs to be done, particularly to tackle recruitment and retention of social workers, to ensure that they are adequately trained in assessment and planning and to improve ways of working across the

social care workforce in line with the cultural and structural changes in the Every Child Matters programme.

7.3 It is also vital that children's care plans are reviewed effectively, and respondents to the consultation made clear that the current independent reviewing mechanism is not working to the benefit of children themselves. Some children also need access to independent adults with whom they can build trusting relationships and interests or to an advocate who can support them if they have a complaint.

Workforce reform

7.4 We will work with partners to develop further proposals for improving three areas of the children's workforce:

a. Remodelling the children's social care workforce;

b. Social worker training and skills; and

c. Social worker recruitment and retention.

7.5 In Autumn 2007, we will set out the Government's vision for the children's workforce in relation to all groups of children – not just those in care – in the planned *Children's Workforce Strategy (CWS) Refresh*. This will build on the Government's *Options for Excellence Review of Social Care*, published in 2006[4], and will include recommendations for improving the skills and knowledge of

---

2 http://www.everychildmatters.gov.uk/deliveringservices/caf/

3 http://www.everychildmatters.gov.uk/deliveringservices/contactpoint/

4 DfES and DH published 'Options for Excellence: Building the Social Care Workforce of the Future' in October 2006. Supporting paper can be found at: http://www.everychildmatters.gov.uk/optionsforexcellence

the social care workforce in each of the three areas outlined above.

Workforce remodelling

7.6 Remodelling the social care workforce means building a modern workforce where education, social care, health and youth justice deliver integrated and multi-agency support to improve outcomes for children and young people. It will help shift the focus towards preventive work, achieve efficiency savings and build a workforce capable of adapting and innovating to meet future needs. In considering future need we will look at new methods, roles, technology, changing demand and service user expectations.

7.7 As part of the strategy to build a world-class children's workforce the Government is helping practitioners across universal, targeted and specialist services to assess children's needs earlier and provide co-ordinated support by setting a common assessment framework; developing lead professionals and developing an integrated qualifications framework to implement a common core of skills across children's professions, supporting progression and workforce mobility. The General Social Care Council (GSCC) is already consulting widely on the roles and tasks of social workers. The outcomes from this consultation will help determine how social work fits into the network of caring services, raise

awareness about its value and identify future needs.

7.8 Key to enabling social workers to spend more time on core work with children is modernising their working tools and environment. We will:

- **Make further funding available in 2008/09 to enhance local authorities' investment in ICT to enable social workers to work flexibly and make more efficient use of time[6], building on the £13 million provided in 2007/08.**

7.9 Alongside this the Children's Workforce Development Council (CWDC) is working with local authorities on social care workforce remodelling as well as supporting the involvement of the private, voluntary and independent sectors.

7.10 To help remodel the social care workforce we will also:

- **Work with the CWDC to set up "remodelling pilots" based on social work teams in about 30 local areas;**

- **Build on the remodelling work already being carried out in local areas by developing practical tools to support dissemination of good practice as well as learning from remodelling that has taken place in schools and the health service;**

- **Learn from international examples of practice on pedagogic**

---

5   This was an early action from the Options for Excellence. The current consultation closes in late June 2007.

6   Guidance for ICT grants http://www.everychildmatters.gov.uk/search/?asset=document&id=59362

approaches to social care in children's services and set up and evaluate a number of pilots in residential care. This action is described in more detail in Chapter 3;

- **Support training for at least two commissioners in every local authority, based on the forthcoming National Occupational Standards for commissioning. This will ensure that commissioners will have the skills to plan local service provision and commission the highest quality services; and**

- **Explore options for setting up a mechanism that brings together the children's social care workforce partners to work on service improvement and modernisation as well as issues around recruitment, retention and skills development.**

Social work training and skills

7.11 We want to improve the skills, training and support for children and family social workers and increase the capacity of social workers to support other social care staff including carers. Carers require effective and timely support, which may include help to access the new qualifications framework. We need a particular focus on: how social workers assess, plan and deliver interventions; the importance of keeping care plans up to date; and better skills for direct

work with children and young people. We will therefore:

- **Review the support offered to newly qualified social workers and to managers and supervisors.**

7.12 We will also look at the social work qualifying degrees to ensure they equip social workers with the knowledge and skills to work in a modern children's workforce, building on the current evaluation of the degree and the forthcoming review of National Occupational Standards for social work. We want to ensure that social work students are properly trained in the tools and experiences they need to do their jobs including: the Integrated Children's System (ICS), safeguarding children procedures, child development theories, working effectively with disabled children and their families and the capacity to deliver evidence based interventions. It is also vital that they are trained to be able to listen effectively to the views of children and young people in care. We will:

- **Explore with partners options for greater child specialisation in the social work qualifying degrees, at undergraduate and postgraduate levels and in post qualifying awards;**

- **Build on the common induction standards that have been developed by the CWDC so that they are adopted across the children's social care workforce;**

- **Commission the CWDC, working with Children's Workforce**

Network (CWN), to research the skills and behaviours required by the children's workforce to support disabled children effectively, as set out in *Aiming High for Disabled Children: Better Support for Families*; and

- **Work with CWDC to establish management induction standards and continue to support the implementation of championing children[7] for managers working in multi-agency settings within the framework of a children's workforce leadership strategy.**

Social Worker recruitment

7.13 In response to what children and young people and those currently in the profession have told us, we want to increase the numbers of skilled social workers in the children's workforce as well as reduce staff turnover and reliance on agency staff. A key aspect of improving recruitment is establishing a positive public image of the profession so that it becomes an attractive career choice in addition to improving career progression options and tackling concerns about stress, excessive workloads and the quality of supervision. We particularly want to review the support and training for newly qualified social workers who may quickly become overloaded, leading to disillusionment and burnout.

7.14 Through Options for Excellence, we are working with the CWDC to support local authorities on workforce planning and at a local level there are many promising examples of good practice. We want to attract people to social work and will learn from work that Skills for Care have undertaken through their Care Ambassadors Scheme in schools which seeks to inspire young people to consider social work as a profession.

7.15 We will therefore:

- **Examine, with partners, options for recruitment campaigns for social workers that are more closely embedded in the context of a children's workforce and the ways of working set out in Every Child Matters;**

- **Look at ways to make the profession more attractive by developing a Newly Qualified Social Worker status that would give a guarantee of support, training and induction to child and family social workers;**

- **Work with GSCC, CWDC and other partners to explore new initial training routes for social workers; and**

---

7   Championing Children is a framework designed to promote a common understanding about the distinctive and different skills, behaviours and knowledge required by managers of children's services who are responsible for multi-agency, multi-professional teams.

- **Clarify the current fit between career pathways for social workers and the post-qualifying awards available to support those pathways.**

Wider roles

7.16 Alongside improvements to the skills and knowledge of social workers, we are developing specific roles with a dedicated focus on children in care. In particular we have established the virtual school head, we are placing designated teachers on a statutory footing (see Chapter 4) and we will set out expectations for health services for children in care (see Chapter 5).

7.17 These roles are intended to ensure that, across all services for children and young people, the authority fulfils its corporate parenting duty in relation to education and health outcomes. They will be responsible for improving the attainment and health of children in care and will support and challenge front line staff, as well as feeding into the strategic decisions being taken locally. For the virtual school head, this involves working with schools to help them fulfil their role in corporate parenting but they must also work with other services across the children's trust.

Social Work Practices

7.18 *Care Matters* put forward social work practices as a new model of social work provision which could potentially offer benefits both to children in care and the professionals who work with them. The proposal offers a new opportunity to enable professionals to work together with greater autonomy and flexibility in order to work more directly with children and young people and better meet their needs. We want to explore whether social work practices would be better at addressing some of the current problems with the care system than current practice in local authorities.

7.19 The Social Care Practices Working Group report sets out a series of recommendations for piloting this model, and encourages the Government to use the term 'social *work* practices' in order to emphasise the key role of qualified professionals in delivering the model. Drawing upon these and other recommendations in the report we will:

- **Legislate to establish a variety of two-year pilots across a diverse range of local authorities to test the social work practice model thoroughly.** The pilots will include social work practices that are run by voluntary and private sector agencies.

7.20 Given the complexity involved in establishing pilots, we will be working closely with local authorities and their representatives (LGA and ADCS) to identify sites for the pilots and to develop indicators for measuring the impact of practices on outcomes for children and on the rest of the care system.

7.21 A practice would be an autonomous organisation, whether a voluntary or community sector organisation, a social enterprise or a private business – similar to a GP practice – registered with OFSTED and responsible for employing social workers. Each practice commissioned by local authorities would fulfil all duties in compliance with statutory social work functions. Each social worker in a practice would have the freedom to concentrate on the children in their care and would be accountable for their outcomes. The practice social worker would remain with them, as far as possible, throughout their time in care and beyond. Each practice would hold a budget provided through the contract with the authority and would use it to enable individual social workers to fund the placement, support and activities that they believe "their children" should have.

7.22 The commissioning local authority would remain the "corporate parent" for all children receiving services through a social work practice and the Director of Children's Services and the Lead Member for Children's Services would continue to be accountable for ensuring that these children achieve and reach their potential.

7.23 In testing the social work practice model, we will want to see whether they offer a way of achieving lower turnover of staff than local authorities; and whether they would result in more time being spent by social workers on relationship-building with children, as well as their impact on the rest of the care system.

7.24 We will also ensure that during the pilots a suitable accountability and regulatory framework is developed to ensure that vulnerable children are protected and are not disadvantaged by the practices.

Getting the basics right – reviewing care plans

7.25 Every child in care must have a care plan based on a comprehensive assessment of their needs that fully takes into account the child's wishes and feelings and aspirations for the future. Care plans should be detailed "live" documents describing the aims and objectives for the child's care – e.g whether they are going to be supported to return to their own family or whether it will only be possible to meet their needs in a permanent substitute family or residential home, and setting out the services required to respond to the full range of every child's needs as they journey through care.

7.26 The care plan should inform the decision as to which placement (e.g. foster care, children's home or placement with family or friends) will best meet the child's needs. Key documents including the Health Plan and Personal Education Plan (PEP) will form an essential part of the overall care plan. It must also include details of the arrangements for maintaining contact between the child and their family and friends, along with clear proposals for supporting the child's sense of identity, addressing any specific cultural, religious or linguistic needs. It will identify particular actions required to meet the needs of a disabled child and set out details of how the child will be supported to enjoy and achieve so that they reach their full potential.

7.27 All care plans must be kept under review. The review process is one of the key components of working with children and families in order to consider the plan for the welfare of the child and monitor the progress in implementing the plan, making decisions to amend it as necessary in light of changed knowledge and circumstances.

Independent Reviewing Officers

7.28 Since September 2004, reviews must be chaired by an Independent Reviewing Officer (IRO) who plays a central role in ensuring that local authority care planning addresses the goals and aspirations of children and young people.

7.29 There is widespread concern that the IRO role is not being carried out effectively across all local authorities and that they are not challenging decisions made by local authorities even in cases where professional practice is obviously poor and not in young people's interests. Not every statutory review is run in a way which encourages a challenging analysis of the proposals for meeting the child's needs. Insufficient weight may be given to the views of the young person or to those of their parents, carers, or other professionals with a role in securing the

child's welfare. Unless care plans are rigorously examined then the review is no longer an opportunity for informed reflection on the child's progress and planning of the child's future; instead, it becomes merely a sterile "box-ticking" exercise.

7.30 One possible solution to this might be to ensure that IRO services are completely independent from the local authority which has statutory responsibility, as the child's corporate parent, for developing and implementing the care plan. However, there are a range of views about this issue and, on balance, it would be premature to pursue the radical option of externalising IRO services to an outside agency – the disruption that this would cause to children in care services in the short term might well outweigh longer term benefits.

7.31 Nevertheless, if the plans outlined below for overhauling and strengthening the IRO role do not support significant improvements in outcomes for children in care, the Government is committed to revisiting this option in future and we will legislate to allow for this possibility.

7.32 In the immediate future we will significantly strengthen the role of the IRO so that each individual IRO is expected to fulfil their role with credibility and independence. They should oversee the care planning process so that it is fair and reasonable and gives proper weight to the child's wishes and feelings, ensuring that local authorities always act as consistent, responsible corporate parents sensitive to the needs of the children and young people in their care.

7.33 To strengthen the role of the IRO, we will:

- **Require local authorities to appoint a named IRO for each child.** This step will enhance the personal accountability and individual responsibilities of each IRO and build in a presumption that every child has a right to a consistent relationship with one professional who keeps their care plan under review;

- **Require IROs to spend time individually with each child prior to any review** so that the IRO personally establishes the child's wishes and feelings about the issues to be covered at the care planning meeting. This requirement will include giving disabled children in care an entitlement either to be supported by an IRO who has been trained in communication and other skills necessary to facilitate care planning for children with significant additional needs or for the IRO to seek a specialist who has these skills to elicit and put forward effectively the child's views;

- **Strengthen existing guidance on the role of IROs by defining a "significant event" when a review must take place before any proposed change can occur for the child.** For example, such changes will include holding a review where there is any proposal that a child should move from a placement regulated by the Care Standards Act (i.e. foster care or a children's homes) to any unregulated placement (e.g. a hostel or, so called, "independent flat"); when any child in care is due to be discharged form custody or a secure children's home; or where placement changes could significantly disrupt plans for the child's education;

- **Update guidance so that a referral by the IRO to The Children and Family Court Advisory and Support Service (CAFCASS) is no longer seen a last resort**, but considered as a real option to ensure proper scrutiny of local authority decisions in cases where individual IROs believe that it is appropriate to escalate their well founded professional concerns; and

- **Amend guidance to specify optimum caseloads for IROs.** At present there is considerable variability between local authorities in the size of IRO caseloads, impeding the effectiveness of some IRO services.

7.33 Strengthening the IRO role will support the transformation that must be achieved to improve outcomes for children in care. An enhanced IRO role will be one keystone to building a culture of responsible corporate parenting so that local authorities listen to children and provide them with a quality personalised service that is genuinely sensitive to their needs and aspirations. IROs are an important source of information for DCSs about the operation of the care planning and reviewing system and there should be systems in place to allow this information to be shared.

Independent Visitors

7.34 Independent visitors are trained volunteers who befriend and support children and young people in care. They give them an opportunity to discuss and explore their ideas, ambitions and concerns, and any issues that they may have. Young people in care often view their Independent Visitor as a friend to talk to – someone who can provide them with emotional support and continuity, as well as enabling them to have fun and share in recreational activities.

7.35 *Care Matters* proposed that independent visitors might be renamed 'independent advocates' in order to recognise some of the excellent work done currently by some independent visitors in representing the views of the children they visit. However, the overwhelming response to this suggestion in consultation was negative: people felt that advocacy is a very distinct role whose purpose should not be confused with 'befriending' or visiting. We have therefore decided not to change the name in this way.

7.36 A number of young people in care – those who have no contact with their parents – are already entitled to an independent visitor. However, independent visitors can potentially benefit a much wider range of children and young people, helping to support placement stability and build constructive relationships and interests, encouraging children and young people's ambitions and aspirations. Children and young people have told us that they would like greater access to the support of an independent visitor. In recognition of this, we will:

- **Legislate to extend the opportunity to have an Independent Visitor to all children in care where they would benefit significantly from such a relationship; and**

- **Revitalise the Independent Visitor scheme by working proactively with local authorities – in partnership with voluntary and private sector organisations – to increase the pool of volunteers who wish to become Independent Visitors.**

Advocacy and complaints

7.37 The reforms set out in this White Paper, including the pledge, workforce reform, and the strengthening of the IRO in particular, are about continuing to create a culture of openness where children and young people are engaged, consulted and involved in decision making. As part of this, **where children in care intend or do make a complaint, local authorities should**

provide access to independent advocacy services in line with the *Get it Sorted* guidance[8]. Local authorities should make sure that this right and the arrangements to support it are well publicised amongst all children and young people, including those with special needs and disabilities.

8   http://www.dfes.gov.uk/childrensadvocacy/docs/GetitSorted.pdf

Chapter 8
Next steps

"Make sure the young people are included and stick to the promises and most of all make changes don't just talk about them."

Young person

Summary

We are determined to harness the enthusiasm and momentum that has built across all parts of the care system during the consultation on the *Care Matters* Green Paper, and we are committed to realising in full the ambitious agenda for transforming the lives of children and young people in care set out in this White Paper.

This chapter sets out:

- **Our plans to strengthen the legislative and regulatory framework underpinning the care system;**

- **The establishment of a national partnership with the voluntary and statutory sectors to lead the implementation of this strategy and ensure outcomes really are transformed for children in care;**

- **Our plans to develop a detailed implementation plan to guide all of us in reaching this vision;**

- **Details of the pilots we are running;**

- **Plans for a change fund to support local authorities and their partners in implementing this White Paper; and**

- **Our approach to working with the private sector to explore how their skills and resources might contribute to improving the life chances of children in care.**

8.1 This White Paper sets out a package of significant change, designed to secure radical improvements in the outcomes of children and young people in care.

8.2 We have started the journey by articulating a clear and bold vision for all children in care. We have worked hard during the consultation on the *Care Matters* Green Paper to engage as many individuals and groups as possible to build the case for new and sustained action. Now, to succeed in really improving the life chances of children in care, we need to build on this good start. We need to harness the enthusiasm, passion and commitment developed during the consultation, to deliver collectively a change programme that will benefit today's children and young people in care and have lasting impact for the future care population.

The right legislative and regulatory framework

8.3 Government has a critical role to play in putting in place the right statutory framework for the care system. The framework should enable children and young people to receive high quality care and support, and drive improvements in the effective delivery of services that are truly focused on the needs of the child. The framework should give local authorities and their partners as much flexibility as possible to respond to local needs and circumstances.

8.4 We will seek the earliest opportunity to amend the current legislative framework around children in care, including:

- Giving pilot local authorities the power to test a different model of organising social care by commissioning services from 'Social Work Practices' (Chapter 7) and enabling regulation of these practices;

- Increasing the focus on the transparency and quality of care planning. This will include putting an even greater emphasis on the voice of the child in care by, for example, strengthening the role of the Independent Reviewing Officer (Chapter 7);

- Increasing schools' capacity to address the particular needs of children in care, including placing the role of the designated teacher on a statutory footing and ensuring that children in care do not move schools in Key Stage 4 except in exceptional circumstances (Chapter 4);

- Improving the quality and stability of placements for children in care, by restricting local authorities from placing out-of-authority, ensuring swift and decisive action can be taken where children's homes are found to be substandard; requiring local authorities to ensure the supply of local provision is sufficient to meet children's needs and ensuring children in care and custody are visited regularly (Chapter 3); and

- Ensuring that young people's views are taken into account when moving towards independence and that they retain support and guidance as long as they need it, including giving young people a greater say over when they move to independent living and raising to age 25 years access for all care leavers to a personal adviser and pathway plan (Chapter 6).

8.5 Alongside these changes we will revise the statutory regulatory framework and statutory guidance. In particular, we will continue our review of the National Minimum Standards (NMS) and underpinning regulations for children's social services made under the Care Standards Act 2000.

8.6 The review of the NMS will put in place a regulatory system that drives up standards of services and works in the best interests of children and young people in care, improving their outcomes. We will do this by putting in place an inspection process that is proportionate to risk, targets inspection where improvement is needed or concerns have been raised and avoids unnecessary burdens on service providers who provide good quality services, while giving the necessary assurance to commissioners of services, service users and their relatives that services are of appropriate quality and safety.

8.7 We have already completed phase one of the NMS review which focused on the statutory minimum inspection frequencies and methodologies for children's social services, following a thorough consultation of our proposals last year. New regulations came into effect on 1 April 2007. In phase two, we will review the standards themselves, working closely with Ofsted, to examine and revise the existing structure and detail of the NMS by 2009. We will set out a detailed timetable for the review in our implementation plan later this year.

8.8 In addition we will consult on revisions to statutory guidance made under the Children Act 1989. We are publishing for consultation alongside this White Paper

a draft version of Volume 1 of the Children Act 1989 statutory guidance. Revision of Volume 1, which covers Court Orders, is a central proposal in the joint *Child Care Proceedings System in England and Wales*, published last year by DCA and DfES. Revision of Volumes 2 – 9 will be now be timetabled to take account of forthcoming legislative changes and this White Paper, for example around introducing the gateway approach to family and friends care described in Chapter 2 and will be published in 2009.

A partnership for delivery

8.9 The responsibility we share for achieving these ambitions for children and young people in care means there must be a shared vision for change. We will construct a partnership-based approach to implementation across the statutory and voluntary sectors.

8.10 The Children's Inter-Agency Group is made up of the key statutory and voluntary organisations delivering services to children. It includes representatives from health, education, social care, and the police, as well as children and young people's voluntary service delivery organisations, and children and youth membership organisations. We want the new joint partnership to be modelled on central government and Children's Inter-Agency Group partners holding each other to account for their respective responsibilities, recognising that we are mutually dependent on each other to transform the whole care system. At a national level we want to provide an exemplar of how we want to see locally owned change.

8.11 Practically we envisage that this joint delivery partnership will:

- build up practical implementation proposals taking account of local capacity issues and construct and monitor a detailed timetable and delivery plan;

- monitor specific milestones for action by both central government and Children's Inter-Agency Group members especially with LGA and ADCS on corporate parenting;

- identify and carry through dissemination opportunities e.g. through conferences and regional events;

- support the roll out of new proposals (e.g. virtual school heads, the pledge) and receive real time feedback from pilot areas; and

- share effective practice and spread it more widely through the Beacon Council Scheme (e.g. children in care councils, the pledge, approaches to corporate parenting, local foster carers recruitment campaigns).

The role of the voluntary sector

8.12 The contribution of the voluntary sector to delivering quality services to children in care has been well-evidenced, and we expect local authorities to give careful consideration to the contribution of local and national voluntary sector organisations in delivering the White Paper.

Working with the private sector

8.13 The private sector, too, has much to offer children in care, particularly helping them to benefit from positive activities as described in Chapter 5, but more broadly in providing access to training and employment opportunities.

8.14 Many major companies already do valuable work to increase vulnerable young people's access to structured leisure activities and other support. We believe children and young people in care will benefit substantially from increased involvement in these programmes, and the outlook is positive: many private firms have been developing a positive track record of engaging directly with children in care.

8.15 As we announced in the *Care Matters* Green Paper, **HSBC** are providing £1m to support private tutoring for children in care, partnering with some of the areas where we are piloting the virtual school head.

8.16 We also believe that children in care should have access to effective routes into employment. **HSBC** and **BT** are leading the way on new work to promote this engagement:

a. We are announcing in this White Paper that **HSBC** will pilot an additional new programme to **provide care leavers with a bridge into their Management Academy**.

b. **BT** offers around 450 new apprenticeships a year and, as part of their commitment to social equity, 30 of these places have been reserved for applicants from families with no record of employment. **BT are committed to increasing the number of care leavers who engage with their apprenticeship programme.** Over the coming months, they will consider the best way of achieving this aim

8.17 We believe that the key to seeing more work like this is to encourage networking between the private sector, the third sector and local authorities so that they can identify where their priorities coincide at a local level across the country. We have begun to work with a number of large national firms to explore partnership opportunities for work with children in care. These companies include **Citi** and **BSkyB**.

8.18 We will facilitate a long-term dialogue between private companies and the care system exploring the potential for building major sponsorship programmes which increase opportunities for children in care across the board.

Resourcing the change programme

8.19 In Chapter 1 we explained that in order to provide further capacity to implement the changes envisaged, we have secured an extra £13.5m in 2007-08 and £89/£96/£107m additional funding (including capital) over 2008-11.

8.20 As part of this envelope we have set aside £22.5m from within the total budget for a change fund to support local authorities in the effective

implementation of *Care Matters* between 2008-11.

8.21 We have published alongside this document a Regulatory Impact Assessment. This includes the funds we are likely to make available to support the delivery of the different policies over the CSR period. This impact assessment is available on the DfES website.

Implementation timetable

8.22 The detailed implementation plan that will be published later in the year will set out in detail our plans for successful implementation and timescales for achieving this. It will also set out a timetable for the legislative changes referred to in this White Paper. The detailed timetable will build on those key milestones already announced.[1]

Drawing on good practice

8.23 The implementation plan will evolve to draw on the experience of local authorities as they embark on implementing local change programmes. We will draw on emerging good practice and in particular the findings of those local authorities piloting effective delivery of key elements of the White Paper, summarised in the table below. In addition, we will support the dissemination of good practice through the Beacon Council Scheme. Local authorities will have the opportunity to seek beacon status later in 2007.

---

1 Details of the costings and equality implications of this White Paper can be found in the Impact Assessment and Equality Impact Assessment on the Every Child Matters website: http://www.everychildmatters.gov.uk

Pilot	Purpose	Commencement	Confirmed LAs
Multi Dimensional Treatment Foster Care	To provide an intensive treatment programme for young children in foster care with complex needs to support future permanent placement	Autumn 06	Dudley, Solihull, North Yorkshire, Manchester, Oxfordshire, West Sussex
Family Drug and Alcohol Court	The model – originally developed in the US – will test out provision of intensive assessment, support, intervention and care plan coordination for families effected by parental substance misuse whose children are in care proceedings	January 08	A single pilot covering Westminster, Islington and Camden
Budget-holding by the lead professional	To pilot social workers having direct access to a budget to purchase services and goods on behalf of the children allocated to their caseload	April 2007	Gateshead, Gloucestershire, Leeds, West Sussex
Regional Commissioning Units	To secure better value for money and give more placement choice for children	September 2007	London, West Midlands, North West, North East, South West, Cross Regional bid based out of Eastern Region
Virtual school head	To look across the educational achievement of children in care across a local authority as if they were in one school with the purpose of providing challenge and support to raise their achievement	September 07	Bournemouth, Cambridgeshire, Dudley, Gateshead, Greenwich, Merton, Norfolk, Salford, Stockport, Walsall and Warwickshire
Private Tutoring (funded by HSBC)	To test out the impact of providing private tutoring for children in care (overseen by the virtual school head)	September 07	Dudley, Merton, Walsall and Warwickshire
Right 2B Cared 4	A pathfinder to test out best practice in ensuring that young people remain in care until 18 unless there are exceptional circumstances and provided with the right kind of support and accommodation for their needs	Autumn 07	Expressions of interest will be sought in Summer 07

Pilot	Purpose	Commencement	Confirmed LAs
Fostering at 18+	To test out allowing care leavers to continue to live with foster families up to the age of 21, to evaluate the support required and the impact on their longer term outcomes	April 08	Expressions of interest will be sought by January 08
Social Work Practices	To test out a model of small groups of social workers undertaking work with children in care commissioned by but independent of local authorities	Autumn 2008 (subject to parliamentary approval)	LAs will be invited to express their interest in piloting Social Work Practices following parliamentary approval LAs wishing to express an early interest in SWPs should contact Mark Burrows (Mark.Burrows@ dfes.gsi..gov.uk)
Children's residential care pedagogy	To fund a pilot programme to evaluate the effectiveness of social pedagogy in residential care	End 2008	Seminar in early July to initiate early conversation with key stakeholders and launch joint report on implementing a pedagogy framework
Multi systemic therapy pilots (in partnership with Department of Health)	To provide an intensive family based intervention to enable high risk adolescents to remain living at home with their families	March 08	Seminar for potential authorities 29 June
Pastoral Care in FE (led by the QIA)	To test out the impact of improved pastoral care for vulnerable groups in FE including children in care	March 07	Bury Camden Dorset Gloucestershire Hackney Hammersmith & Fulham Herefordshire Hertfordshire Newham Nottinghamshire Somerset Suffolk Westminster Worcestershire

Printed in the UK for The Stationery Office Limited
on behalf of the Controller of Her Majesty's Stationery Office
ID5596874   06/07
Printed on Paper containing 75% recycled fibre content minimum.